White Line Fever

An Illustrated History of Irish Road Racing

White Line Fever

An Illustrated History of Irish Road Racing

Alastair McCook

Gill & Macmillan

Gill & Macmillan Ltd

Hume Avenue, Park West, Dublin 12

with associated companies throughout the world

www.gillmacmillan.ie

© Alastair McCook 2006

ISBN-13: 978 07171 4085 5

ISBN-10: 0 7171 4085 7

Design and print origination by Design Image

Colour reproduction by Typeform Repro

Printed and bound by L.E.G.O. Spa, Italy

This book is typeset in 9pt on 14pt humanist.

The paper used in this book comes from the wood pulp of managed forests.

For every tree felled, at least one tree is planted, thereby renewing natural resources.

A CIP catalogue record for this book is available from the British Library.

1 3 5 4 2

CONTENTS

Dedication

This book is dedicated to my wife Ruth, my girls Annie and Holly, and my son Ben.

It is also dedicated to the memory of two of our finest road racers, Richard Britton who lost his life as the result of a racing accident at Ballybunion in 2005, and Darran Lindsay who was killed twelve months later during practice for the Killalane road races in September 2006.

Acknowledgments

This book would not have been possible without the help of the following people:

Esler Crawford, Dick Creith, Susan Dalzell, Graham Houlihan, Ben McCook, Ruth McCook, Barbara McIntyre, Derek McIntyre, Clifford McLean, Bob May, Elwyn Roberts, Norman Waddell, Theresa Wisener.

A special "thank you" is owed to Douglas James at Bennett's Photo Lab, Ballymoney. Thanks for all your help and hard work.

Front Jacket Photograph

Isle of Man TT 2000. Joey Dunlop gets down to the serious task of winning the Formula 1 TT.
On his way past the Highlander on the SP1 VTR 1000 Works Honda.
Photo: Alastair McCook

Back Jacket Photograph

Guy Martin gets the Robinson Honda airborne on one of road racing's most spectacular jumps, nudging past 150 mph at Kells, Co. Meath, 2005.
Photo: Alastair McCook

Introduction

This book is a celebration of the sport of Irish motor cycle road racing. It is a tribute to the riders who are our heroes, the men who first inspired myself and many, many others to lift a camera and try to record the incredible skill and bravery of the road racers. The book is equally a tribute to the art of the many motor cycle photographers who showed us what great photographs look like, and that nearly anything is possible with just a camera body, a lens and a simple roll of film. They have produced some of the most enduring and evocative sporting images ever seen.

In the modern era the digital format is the preferred medium for the majority of photographers, and the new technology has pushed back the boundaries and encouraged many new names to take photographs. Having said that, all the images in this book were taken on conventional print or slide film. From my own point of view old habits die hard and there are certain types of film I love to use, and I suppose as long as they are still made, I'll continue to buy them.

The book covers 60 years in the history of a sport where the highs are like nothing else and the lows can be devastating. The very nature of road racing is inherently dangerous and despite the efforts of race organizers in recent years to minimize the risks and remove hazards, it remains a part of the basic fabric of the sport. Racing motor cycles capable of speeds of over 200 mph on closed, public country roads is never going to be completely safe, and sadly accidents happen, sometimes with tragic consequences.

Despite the dangers most road races attract more entries than there are places on grids. The 60 years that are covered in this book have produced more than their fair share of superhuman feats and deeds, races and riders whose names have already been written large in legend. Names like Bell, Armstrong, Creith, Bryans, Dunlop, McCallan and Farquhar bring to mind memories of greatness, of men who have danced on the edge of danger, who have defied the odds in pushing themselves and their machines to the very edge in their quest for speed and glory. The fans who turn out to line the hedges and road sides in their thousands, rain or shine, share the passion that inspires the men and women in leathers and helmets who brave the risks. It is a mutual passion that makes the heart beat a little faster, that makes the palms of your hands sticky with sweat, that makes the very breath catch in your chest. It is White Line Fever. There is no known cure.

ROADS CLOSE AT 11 A.M. — RACE STARTS AT 12 NOON

ULSTER GRAND PRIX
CLADY CIRCUIT · 20th AUGUST, 1949

21st CLASSIC INTERNATIONAL
PROMOTED BY · THE ULSTER MOTOR CYCLE CLUB LTD.
HELD UNDER THE INTERNATIONAL COMPETITION RULES OF THE F.I.C.M.
AND THE OPEN COMPETITION RULES OF THE MOTOR CYCLE UNION OF IRELAND, ULSTER CENTRE

OFFICIAL SOUVENIR PROGRAMME   2/-

BEST DESCRIPTIONS AND
PHOTOGRAPHS WILL BE IN NEXT WEEK'S THE

1940s

The first road race held after the end of World War II took place at Bangor Castle Demesne, Co. Down, when the Ards Motor Cycle Club ran a 3-race programme on 14th July 1945 over the 1.025-mile circuit. Out of a total of 35 entrants, 25 men and machines made it to the starting line and fought it out for the honours in the Novice, Semi Expert and Expert Classes before a sun-kissed crowd of over 20,000.

Pictured getting away at the start of the Experts race are 27 Ernie Lyons (Triumph), the Flying Farmer from Kill, Co. Kildare, and 28 Belfast's Artie Bell (Norton). The two Irish riders were destined to play a starring role in motor cycle racing in the remaining years of the 1940s. Both would serve the mighty Norton factory as works riders. Lyons spent a miserable time in the employment of the Bracebridge concern during the 1947 season, before eventually being replaced by Ken Bills. It was a low point in Lyons' career and contrasted sharply with the all-conquering performances that had brought him a famous win in appalling conditions at the 1946 Manx Grand Prix, as well as an International victory at the 1939 North West 200.

In contrast Artie Bell's years as a Norton rider were the best of his all-too-short career. In 1947 Bell notched up wins at two of the most prestigious meetings on the calendar, the 500cc Dutch TT at Assen and his home Grand Prix on the gruelling Clady circuit. He won the 1948 Senior TT by over ten minutes and tasted success again in Switzerland with a 350cc win. A classy performance at a rain-drenched Assen in 1949 sealed an unbroken hat trick of consecutive wins at the Dutch TT. And then, with Bell poised to make his claim on the 500cc world crown in 1950, fate dealt its cruellest blow. Whilst battling for the lead in the Belgian Grand Prix Bell sustained injuries that ended his career after crashing with Carlos Bandirola and Les Graham.

Photo: Alastair McCook Photo Archive

14 Cromie McCandless, 24 T Seymour (500cc Rudge), 21 J Nesbitt (490cc Rudge), and 13 G McQueen (498cc Triumph) push off as the Semi Experts race gets underway at Bangor Castle, 14th July 1945. McCandless won the race riding what *Motor Cycling Magazine* (26th July 1945) described as a "rear-sprung Triumph Special". In actual fact the machine that carried McCandless to victory that day was the prototype, the working blueprint and design for the legendary Featherbed Norton, and referred to by the McCandless brothers as "The Benial" (Latin for The Beast).

The Featherbed was the brainchild of the older of the two McCandless brothers, Rex, and pointed the direction of racing motor cycle design for generations. That sunny day in July in front of the thousands who emerged from the shadow cast by six years of war, the McCandless brothers set fastest laps on their inspired creation, Cromie in the Semi Experts, and Rex on his way to a third-place finish in the Experts Class.

In the years ahead the Featherbed design would maintain Norton as a contender against the challenge of the Italian multis, and in the hands of Duke and Bell would prove an irresistible combination as the 1940s merged into the 1950s.

Ernie Lyons recalled the sight of the McCandless "Special" at Bangor during an interview in 2000:

"I raced against it at Bangor Castle in 1945, it was the first race after the war. It was the prototype of all racers. Rex wasn't a graduate engineer, he learned the hard way. He was tremendously logical, he'd argue something and go back to the basics and start building it up from the start. He realized at a very early stage that the bicycle-type frame was never rigid enough, with the weight of the engine swinging out of it on fast bends. That machine deserved to be in a museum."

Photo: Alastair McCook Photo Archive

First held in 1925 by the North Down Club, the Carrowdore 100 with its traditional date in September each year provided the finale to the racing season for many years. The Belfast and District Club took over the running of the race in 1927 and remained in charge up until 2000 when the race was last held. In its latter years the Carrowdore provided some memorable encounters but proved too dangerous as a venue after top riders Eddie Sinton and Tony Carey lost their lives whilst racing at Carrowdore.

The photographs on pages 4 and 5 were taken during the 1946 Carrowdore 100 when the meeting was still run over the $7\frac{1}{2}$-mile circuit on a handicap basis. In the absence of Ernie Lyons from the starting line-up the scratch men that day were Artie Bell and Terry Hill, both conceding time to the entire field who started before them. The limit men (ie the riders who were allowed the most generous handicap), A F Tocher and W J Noble, set off a full $29\frac{1}{2}$ minutes ahead of Bell and Hill.

Hill's challenge for the win was effectively ended on the first lap when he lost over five minutes after stopping for running repairs. Bell (pictured above) on the other hand mounted a stern challenge, posting fastest laps with monotonous regularity, finally clocking a best time of 76.52 mph. It was still only enough for the Belfast star to finish in fourth place.

Photo: Alastair McCook Photo Archive

45 Bill Nicholson (348cc BSA) and 46 Harry Turner (348cc Norton) scorch through the start/finish during their tooth-and-nail battle at the 1946 Carrowdore 100. A single second divided them on the road for the final two laps of the race, but in the end they finished in this order claiming fourth and fifth place respectively.

Photo: Alastair McCook Photo Archive

Twelve months later and the venue changes to the Temple 100, where the handicap system was no less severe. Once again W J Noble was the recipient of a generous allowance, setting off 28½ minutes ahead of the rider on scratch, one W A C McCandless. 30 McCandless pictured on his 499 Norton had the consolation of setting a fastest lap of 67.49 mph but did not finish the race.

The Temple was the longest established race held in the British Isles apart from the Isle of Man TT races. Despite the fact that the necessary legislation to allow public roads to be closed for the purpose of car and motor cycle racing did not exist in Ireland before 1922, the first Temple meeting was staged over a 25-mile course in 1921. The Temple soon established a reputation as one of the great, pure road races and amongst a distinguished list of past winners names like Herbie Chambers, Walter Rusk, Tommy Robb, Ray McCullough, Dick Creith, Tom Herron, Phillip McCallan, and Robert and Joey Dunlop bear testimony to the event's pedigree. One of the most memorable races seen over the Temple course took place in 1970 when Seeley-mounted Denis Gallagher and local ace Gerry Mateer (Norton) went head to head in the 500cc race. At the line the judges couldn't split them and both riders were credited with the same race average of 86.09 mph and the result declared a dead heat.

In latter years the Temple established a reputation verging on notorious due to the challenging nature of the course which gave little room for error.

The Temple 100 was last run on 31st July 1999 with Owen McNally winning the final race staged on the circuit, the 125cc race. The meeting was abandoned after local rider Philip Conroy sustained fatal injuries after crashing out of the Support race. It was the last time the Temple 100 would appear on the road racing calendar.

Photo: Alastair McCook Photo Archive

Brendan Barry-Walshe (490 Norton) had no more luck than Cromie McCandless during the 1947 Temple 100. Barry-Walshe was another non-finisher after crashing at Drumalig Corner. The 1947 Temple 100 was the first to be held since 1936. The prohibitive cost of insurance and the outbreak of World War II had prevented the event from taking place.

Photo: Alastair McCook Photo Archive

W J Spratt's 490cc Triumph is wheeled away as he retires from the 1948 Ulster. Behind him the Norton team, with Joe Craig with his back to the camera, gather round factory runner Louis Carter as he seeks solace from the unrelenting rain. W J "Willie" Spratt began his racing career in the 1930s, before serving in India and Burma with the RAF during World War II. He retired in 1969 after making his final appearance at the Skerries 100.

On this occasion Spratt's race ended in retirement whilst Carter rejoined the fray to claim fourth place in the 350cc race.

Photo: Alastair McCook Photo Archive

Run in appalling conditions, the 1948 Ulster Grand Prix was awarded the prestigious title of Grand Prix d'Europe for the second time in its history. The finest road racers in the world defied the worst nature could muster and battled into the teeth of a gale and through the driving rain. The 350cc 13-lapper took over 2½ hours to complete and ended in a flag-to-flag victory for Freddie Frith riding Nigel Spring's Velocette. Frith, seen here leading the entire field off the grid whilst riding without hands as he adjusts his goggles, led the entire race distance to head an all-Velocette top three of Ken Bills and Frank Fry. Heading the pack as they leave the grid is 42 Manliff Barrington (Norton). Frith confirmed his mastery of the 350cc class by claiming the first world title in 1949.

Photo: Alastair McCook Photo Archive

9

With the crowd long gone and the race over, riders, mechanics and race officials remain, soaked to the bone and frozen after the 1948 Ulster Grand Prix. Amongst the machines still at their pit are the 350cc Velocette of O S Scott, and the mounts of 92 E Stevens and 93 Stan Millar.

Photo: Alastair McCook Photo Archive

1950s

Pits and scoreboard at the end of the last Ulster
Grand Prix to be held on the Clady circuit in 1952.

Photo: Alastair McCook Photo Archive

Bill Webster refuels machine and rider during his pit stop in the 250cc 1950 Ulster Grand Prix. Nicknamed "Websterini" because of his close links with the Italian factories and particularly MV, Bill Webster had a long and successful career racing on the continental Grands Prix circus and Isle of Man TT. His career-best result came at the age of 46 in the 1956 Ulster Grand Prix when he claimed third place in the 125cc race behind Ubbiali and Ferri.

Photo: Alastair McCook Photo Archive

One of the finest riders to come out of Italy, Umberto Masetti prepares for battle prior to the 1950 500cc Ulster, whilst Gilera team manager Piero Taruffi looks on. Whilst Geoff Duke took the win Masetti failed to finish in the top three, but ended the season as world champion. Masetti's finest moment at Clady came the following year when he claimed third place behind the Nortons of Duke and Kavanagh. The Italian legend added a second 500cc world title in 1952.

Photo: Alastair McCook Photo Archive

After racing for 214½ miles on the limit over Clady's unforgiving bumps, this is all that separated the all-Norton-mounted battle for second place at the end of the 1951 350cc Ulster Grand Prix. Ken Kavanagh stole past the flag with his nose just in front of his team mate Johnny Lockett to nick the verdict.

The newspaper headlines proclaimed the genius of Geoff Duke who won both the 500cc and 350cc races at the meeting. Kavanagh followed Duke home for the runner-up spot in both events but at the end of the season it was Lockett who held second place behind Duke in the 350cc world title chase. Kavanagh's finest hour at the Ulster came two years later when he romped home to a famous 500cc victory on the first running of the 'Prix over the Dundrod circuit.

Photo: Alastair McCook Photo Archive

Umberto Masetti and Nello Pagani leave scrutineering and prepare to uphold the honour of Gilera and Italy prior to the start of the 1951 Ulster Grand Prix. Masetti (nearest the camera, pulling on his gloves) finished third in the race, and ended the season in third place behind Duke and Milani in the 500cc world championship. Pagani had the distinction of claiming the inaugural 125cc world championship in 1949. Masetti was one of racing's true greats, listing amongst his many achievements the 1950 and 1952 500cc world titles.

Photo: Alastair McCook Photo Archive

Duke and Kavanagh defy the driving rain as they set off side by side, with the rest of the 1951 Ulster Grand Prix 500cc grid already trailing behind them. After more than two and a half hours and a distance of 247½ miles in truly appalling conditions Duke claimed the win, finishing three minutes ahead of Kavanagh. Also pictured are 10 Reg Armstrong, 17 Nello Pagani and 3 Jack Brett.

Photo: Alastair McCook Photo Archive

This is the start of the last 500cc Grand Prix to be run over the Clady circuit. The front rows consisted of an exotic blend of Nortons, MV, AJS and Gileras, all factory prepared and supported machinery ridden by the best in the world. Notably THE finest rider in the world at that time, Geoff Duke, is missing. He had suffered a broken leg after crashing at Schotten during the German Grand Prix but the line-up still makes mouth-watering reading.

From left they are: 5 Umberto Masetti (Gilera), 10 Jack Brett (AJS), 6 Alfredo Milani (Gilera), 4 Ken Kavanagh (Norton), 35 John Surtees (Norton), 12 Bill Lomas (MV), 27 Dickie Carter (Norton), and 1 Reg Armstrong (Norton).

Lomas finished in third place behind Rod Coleman (AJS) and race-winner Cromie McCandless (Gilera).

Photo: Alastair McCook Photo Archive

Bill Lomas' MV is fettled prior to the start of the 1952 Ulster Grand Prix. Lomas finished in third place in a race decimated by retirements, whilst Cromie McCandless headed Rod Coleman home to take the win.

Photo: Alastair McCook Photo Archive

Twenty-nine-year-old works Gilera rider Giuseppe Colnago pits to refuel his 500-4 during the 1952 Ulster. Colnago's ride at Clady on the day ended in mechanical failure, but he rode with distinction for Gilera on many occasions, listing wins at Siracusa, Senigallia and Faenza during the 1953 season as career highlights. Colnago's greatest moment was undoubtedly his victory at the Belgian Grand Prix in 1955. After riding for Gilera Colnago moved to the Moto Guzzi factory and scored a memorable victory at Siracusa in 1957 riding the legendary 500cc V-8 Guzzi.

Photo: Alastair McCook Photo Archive

Jack Brett rode his heart out for fifteen laps of the 1953 350cc Ulster Grand Prix and ended up with nothing to show for his heroics. In the end victory went to Ken Mudford, but Brett showed true grit as he fought tooth and nail to keep a grasp on a place on the podium whilst the likes of Alano Montanari, Bob McIntyre and Derek Farrant did their utmost to earn a podium finish. Brett, pictured in the pits on his works Norton, was forced to retire at Tullyrusk. A third-place finish behind Kavanagh and Duke in the 500cc race offered some consolation for Brett.

Photo: Alastair McCook Photo Archive

The Sidecar Class was first included in the Ulster Grand Prix programme in 1953. The new venture only attracted a field of seven outfits, but produced a memorable battle between Cyril Smith and Eric Oliver that was only decided on the final lap when Oliver's engine seized. Smith took the win with two minutes to spare from Pip Harris. Pictured at the off are: 1 Pip Harris (Norton/Watsonian), 6 Jacques Drion (Norton/Watsonian), 3 Eric Oliver (Norton/Watsonian), 2 Fron Purslow (BSA), 7 E Walker (Norton/Watsonian).

Photo: Alastair McCook Photo Archive

Reg Armstrong's record as a rider competing at the top level of motor cycle road racing is simply outstanding. Between 1949 and 1955 Armstrong finished runner-up in the world championships on five occasions. In 1949 riding a Velocette he finished as 350cc runner-up, an achievement he repeated in 1952 whilst riding for Norton. He also claimed third place in the 1952 500cc title chase. The following year Armstrong switched to Gilera and finished in second place in the 500cc table, as well as taking the 250cc runner-up spot as a works NSU rider. Armstrong's final world championship runner-up finish came in the 500cc class in 1955, finishing behind his Gilera team mate Geoff Duke.

Pictured on his way to victory on the factory Gilera at the 1954 Leinster 200.

Photo: Elwyn Roberts Collection

In 1957 the Mid Antrim 150 was still held over the fast, 10.4-mile Ballygarvey circuit. The race had been first run over a 6-mile circuit at Ballygarvey in 1946 before switching to the longer 10.4-mile track the following year. The Mid Antrim 150 switched to the shorter 5.7-mile Rathkenny circuit in 1965, and by then the event was staged on a Saturday, for obvious and very good reasons. In 1957 the Mid Antrim was still held mid-week on a Wednesday and still run on a handicap basis.

Making the headlines was Norton-mounted Banbridge star Wilfie Herron, the scratch man on the day, who came within a whisker of posting the first 100-mph lap in the history of the race. Herron could only finish sixth overall in the Open Handicap event, losing four minutes on handicap to eventual winner J McGimpsey. Herron had the consolation of winning the 500cc class from ex-footballer Jimmy Jones. In later years Wilfie's nephew Tom dominated the sport at home and abroad up until his death in 1979.

Photo: Bob May

Manx invader Jackie Wood rounds Church Corner in front of a full house as he coaxes his 500cc Norton towards Portstewart in the 1957 North West 200. It was a historic occasion after race-winner Jack Brett posted the first 100-mph lap ever recorded at the event. Brett took the win with ease, finishing over seven minutes ahead of runner-up Ken Patrick. Brett added the 1957 500cc third place to his 1955 350cc North West 200 victory.

Photo: Esler Crawford

IRELAND'S N.-W. '200'

PRESS

1958

N. I. M. C.

IRELAND'S N.-W. "200"

PRESS

1956

Before 1939 the supercharged BMWs in the hands of the likes of Jock West and George Maier were formidable opposition no matter who you were. After the end of World War II the German factory never enjoyed anything like the success they had previously enjoyed. It wasn't for the want of employing the services of star-name riders like Dickie Dale, pictured above with a works mechanic at the 1958 Ulster Grand Prix. Dale teamed up with German star Eric Hiller (right) in the BMW team, and finished the '58 season in third place behind John Surtees and John Hartle in the 500cc points table. In the modern era BMW will be mostly remembered for their dominance of the Sidecar Class in the hands of riders like Noll, Schneider, Camathias, Scheidegger, Fath and Enders.

Photos: Esler Crawford

The might of the Italian MV factory on display for all to see at Dundrod in 1959. On race day John Surtees stormed to a 350cc/500cc double, whilst team mate John Hartle posted the fastest lap of the 350cc race before retiring after hitting the bank at Tornagrough.

Photo: Esler Crawford

CARROWDORE 3½
NEWTOWNARDS 9¾

BELFAST 19¾

1960s

The AJS-mounted pair of 32 Bob McIntyre and 20 Alan Shepherd battle it out through Church Corner for the North West 200 350cc race win during their hectic encounter on the Triangle in 1960. It was a good day for Shepherd who snuck past the brilliant Scot on the final bend to take a famous win by one fifth of a second. Shepherd also claimed a 500cc third place whilst McIntyre's challenge for Senior honours ended in retirement after his oil tank split.

Photo: Esler Crawford

OFFICIAL PROGRAMME 2s 6d

33rd CLASSIC INTERNATIONAL

ULSTER GRAND PRIX

DUNDROD CIRCUIT
NORTHERN IRELAND
12 AUGUST 1961

MOTORCYCLE

YOUR FASTEST WAY TO THE FACTS · THURSDAY 4d

After the 1960 season MV abandoned their involvement in the smaller classes and channelled their efforts into pursuing the 350cc and 500cc world titles with Rhodesian star Gary Hocking in the saddle of the Italian machines. Hocking duly delivered the goods, securing both titles for the Italian factory. Pictured on the 500cc MV during an emphatic trouncing of the opposition at Dundrod in 1961 where the Hocking/MV combination headed the 350s and 500s home.

The fact that the Rhodesian from Bulawayo won seven out of nine 500cc Grands Prix that he contested in 1961 underlines his dominance of the sport at that time. However, everything changed for Hocking after his close friend and rival, Tom Phillis, was killed after crashing at Laurel Bank on the second lap of the 1962 Junior TT. Hocking finished six seconds behind Mike Hailwood to take second place in the race, and two days later won the Senior TT. However, his racing career on two wheels was over and Hocking immediately informed the MV factory that he was retiring from the sport.

Hocking switched to racing on four wheels and claimed pole position in his first race, driving a Lotus in a Formula Libre race at Mallory Park. He took his first race win in October 1962 at the South African Kyalami Rand Spring Trophy in October '62, and seemed to get faster with each successive drive at circuits such as Zwartkops and Kumalo in his native Rhodesia. Tragically Gary Hocking lost his life when his Lotus 24 flipped at the South African circuit of Westmead in December 1962.

Photo: Esler Crawford

29

The sound of screaming two-stroke engines fill the air as Kuminitsu Takahashi (Honda) just about remains out of the clutches of Tom Phillis (Honda), Ernest Degner (MZ), Jim Redman (Honda), and Mike Hailwood (Honda) as they swoop beneath the trees at Irelands and on towards Budore during the 1961 125cc Ulster Grand Prix. Takahashi took the win for Honda after an epic battle with Degner (MZ) and Phillis following him home, but it would be Tom Phillis who claimed the Tiddler crown at the end of the season. Takahashi's achievement is unique — he remains the only Japanese winner at the Ulster Grand Prix.

Photo: Esler Crawford

The works 250cc Hondas provided a truly spectacular sight, sound and smell as they flash through Irelands in formation during the 1961 250cc Ulster Grand Prix. Tom Phillis leads the charge from Hailwood and Redman. The Japanese factory filled the first four places in the Quarter Litre Class, with Bob McIntyre taking his only Ulster Grand Prix win after setting a new lap record of 96.94 mph. Behind the hard-charging Scot, Hailwood had the edge over Redman and Phillis. During Dundrod's heady days as a round of the world championship the finest riders and machines graced Co. Antrim's country roads. We will never see its like again.

Photo: Esler Crawford

Following the great MV riders who had gone before him like Hocking and Surtees, men who had dominated the 500cc class on the exotic Italian "Fire Engines", Mike Hailwood, possibly the greatest of all of them, came to Dundrod in 1962 equipped with the finest machinery from Meccanica Verghera's workshops. It would prove to be a day of mixed fortunes for Hailwood. In the 350cc race Hailwood had pushed the lap record to 95.08 mph, in an effort to shake off the challenge of Jim Redman. When the 350cc MV dropped a valve Hailwood had no option but to surrender, tour to the pits and retire.

The 500cc race was a different matter entirely, with Hailwood streaking into an instant lead which he held to the flag. At the end the Maestro had pulverised the lap record, pushing it to 99.99 mph and lapping the entire field up to third-place finisher Phil Read.

Photos: Alastair McCook Photo Archive

With Tommy Robb already out of sight and on the way to taking his maiden Grand Prix on his home circuit, the field streams away at the start of the 1962 250cc Ulster Grand Prix. They are: eventual runner-up 2 Jim Redman (Honda), 10 Hugh Anderson (Suzuki), 22 Dan Shorey (Bultaco), 28 Arthur Wheeler (Moto Guzzi) and 12 Frank Perris (Suzuki).

Photo: Esler Crawford

John Williams was the first rider to win three races in a day at the North West 200, but Alan Shepherd came damn close to becoming the event's first hat-trick man in 1962. In the 350cc and 500cc races Shepherd was untouchable, but couldn't match veteran Arthur Wheeler's speed or experience in the 250cc race. Wheeler won his first North West 200 riding a Velocette in 1951, and eleven years later and Moto Guzzi-mounted he was still setting lap records and winning races at Portstewart. Pictured on the 500cc Matchless Shepherd rounds Church Corner, well clear of Raymond Spence and Billy McCosh.

Photo: Esler Crawford

The Carter brothers, Louis and Dickie, excelled as road racers of the highest calibre. This is one of Dickie Carter's finest moments, rounding Metropole Corner at Portrush on the 250cc NSU on his way to third place behind Arthur Wheeler and Alan Shepherd in 1962. It was his second podium finish in the race in two years. In 1961 Carter finished runner-up behind Tommy Robb and ahead of Arthur Wheeler in the 250cc North West 200.

Photo: Esler Crawford

Rush hour at Ballywalter Corner during the 1962 Carrowdore 100: 55 Charlie Watts (350cc Norton), 57 D Shelton (350cc AJS), 58 Ken Turner (350cc AJS), 65 N F Sweetman (350cc BSA), 62 W McManus (350cc AJS), 63 T Harley (BSA), 66 George Rodgers (BSA).

Photo: Unknown

Harris Healey in action during the 1963 Skerries 100 exiting the Railway Bridge as Denis Gallagher gives chase. In more recent times Healey has worked as an administrator in the sport, serving as Chair of the Motor Cycle Union of Ireland, Ulster Centre in 1986 and 1987, and as President in 1988 and 1989.

Photo: Bob May

Austin Kinsella (174cc Moto Guzzi) and Owen Sheridan (248cc NSU) round Kelly's Pub corner during the 1964 Leinster 200. The photo couldn't have been taken anywhere else but in Ireland — crowds lining the verges of the roads, Gardaí supervising the mayhem and men drinking porter in the pub whilst keeping one eye on the action on the other side of the window.

Austin Kinsella is remembered as a tenacious competitor on his home roads circuits, but he also made his mark in endurance racing. In 1968 Kinsella partnered Ken Buckmaster on a 650cc Triumph Bonneville at the Barcelona 24-hour race held at Montjuich Park. In 1970 Kinsella, Buckmaster and their Triumph returned to Barcelona to once again claim the runner-up spot. The Kinsella/Buckmaster partnership ended the 1970 season in second place overall in the FIM Coupe d'Endurance.

Photo: Esler Crawford

No rider had won a race at the North West 200 on a Japanese machine before Honda-mounted Ralph Bryans swept the boards with an all-conquering 250cc/350cc double in 1964. It was a good day out for the Irish at the seaside: Dick Creith, Bryan's close friend, claimed a famous 500cc victory. Pictured at full cry on the 350cc Honda on Portstewart promenade.

Photo: Ralph Bryans Collection

Dick Creith's place in the folklore of Irish motor cycle racing history is richly deserved. In a career that lasted from 1958 to 1965 his achievements are enough to fill a book in their own right, but the highlights most definitely were back-to-back North West 200 wins in 1964 and 1965, and his legendary victory in the rain at the 1965 Ulster Grand Prix. If the 1964 500cc race had been a lap longer then the likelihood is that Creith would have gone one better than his second-place finish behind Phil Read.

This photograph shows the Bushmills star after another successful day, the occasion being the 1964 Carrowdore 100 where he set fastest lap, claimed the 500cc race win from Bill McCosh and bagged the 100-mile Irish 500cc title into the bargain. Also in the picture are Creith's sponsor, Joe Ryan, and helper, Robbie Taggart (in waterproof coat with back to the camera). Not a bad day's work by any standards.

Photo: Esler Crawford

39

INFORMATION AND TICKET BOOKING FORM

35th
Classic International

Ulster Grand Prix

DUNDROD CIRCUIT

BELFAST

SATURDAY, 10th AUGUST, 1963

Billy McCosh is remembered as one of the finest Irish riders to grace a race track. The Ballymena man began racing in the late 1950s and continued in the saddle well into the 1970s. McCosh was a stalwart of the Isle of Man TT races where he made his début in 1960 and his last appearance in 1974. He finished in the top ten on four occasions on The Island, including consecutive sixth places in the 1964 and 1965 Senior TTs, Matchless-mounted on both occasions.

On home soil McCosh's biggest rival was Dick Creith, and he is pictured here on his way to victory in the 1964 500cc race at the Killinchy 150, after an intense battle between the two ended in a rare mechanical failure for Creith. On the day McCosh claimed the 350cc runner-up spot, sandwiched between Len Ireland and Ian McGregor.

Photo: Esler Crawford

Two of the finest road racers of the 1960s at their work during the 1965 Leinster 200 on the Dunboyne circuit. Manx hero Sid Mizen leads Bushmills' Dick Creith into the Sheaf of Wheat Hairpin as the crowd look on from every available vantage point including the roof tops. The day ended with honours even, with Mizen and Creith taking a win each. Creith retired at the end of the '65 season, Mizen lost his life after crashing at Le Mans in April 1966.

Photo: Ralph Bryans Collection

As a youngster Len Ireland watched his first motor cycle race, the 1947 Ulster Grand Prix, and was immediately hooked. Ireland began his own illustrious career riding a 350cc Manx Norton at the 1958 Tandragee 100. Luck never favoured Ireland at the big international meetings on home soil, but he won at virtually every other track in Ireland, as well as claiming silver replica finishes in the Isle of Man, and respectable performances at circuits such as Mallory, Snetterton and Aintree. A massive crash at the Deers Leap during the 1967 Ulster Grand Prix almost ended Ireland's career, but he fought back from serious injuries to once again taste success. Len Ireland retired in 1970 after making his final appearance riding an Aermacchi at Lurgan Park.

Pictured in full flight on Temple's infamous jumps in 1965 on his way to third place in the 500cc race behind Sid Mizen and Dick Creith. On the day Ireland claimed the 350cc runner-up spot behind his great friend and rival Creith. Len Ireland's only Temple 100 win came via a 350cc victory in 1964.

Photo: Esler Crawford

Sidecars have provided some unforgettable memories in the years since they first graced Dundrod's twisting roads in 1953. The sidecar men and women are a special breed, placing absolute trust between driver and passenger, thinking and moving as one person as they skim the grass banks and hedges, demonstrated here by the partnership of N J Taylor and W Kirkwood as they round Tornagrough on their 650cc Triumph during the 1966 Killinchy 150. The Sidecar Class was discontinued from the Ulster Grand Prix after an accident during the warm-up lap in 1997 claimed the lives of competitor Stephen Galligan and seven-year-old spectator Christopher McConnell-Hewitt.

Photo: Esler Crawford

Tommy Robb's name will always be synonymous with the Grand Prix glory days of the 1960s when he proved on the circuits of the world that he was as good as the best in the business when the opposition comprised men like Hailwood, Agostini, Bryans, Redman and Taveri. Robb moved from top privateer-riding for sponsors like Terry Hill and Geoff Monty to carrying the flag for Honda, Yamaha and Bultaco as a works Grand Prix rider. In 1962 Robb finished in third place in both the 125cc and 350cc world championships, highlights in a career littered with success.

His Leinster 200 win in 1966 was one of Tommy's more unexpected victories, and no one was more surprised at the finish than Robb. After his 250cc Bultaco broke a crank pin during practice Robb worked through the night, and with repairs hastily completed and no time to spare, the Belfast man came under starter's orders with little hope that his machine would last the distance. He had nothing to worry about — on his way to claiming the race win from Billy McCosh, Robb pushed the lap record that had been set by Bob McIntyre in 1961 to 92.90 mph. One of Ireland's truly great road racers.

Photo: Esler Crawford

The 350cc grid lines up before the start of the 1967 Tandragee 100. Nearest the camera is 4 Len Ireland (348cc Norton), 3 Bill McCosh (348cc AJS), 2 Bob Steele (348cc AJS), 1 Ian McGregor (348cc Norton), and 5 Denis Gallagher (350cc AJS).

Photo: May Fox

Mike Hailwood won his first Grand Prix at Dundrod, riding a little Ducati in the 125cc race in 1959. Hailwood's final appearance at the Ulster in 1967 was no less successful. Hailwood was in a different class contesting both 500cc and 250cc races and winning both. Hailwood ended the '67 season as 250cc/350cc World Champion, but a golden era was already over. Honda withdrew from Grand Prix racing at the end of the season, and although Hailwood's career had many glory days to come in the years ahead, his domination of the Grand Prix circus was also over.

Photo: Esler Crawford

World-champion-in-waiting Bill Ivy keeps an eye on the opposition, his factory Yamaha team mate Phil Read, as they exit the Hairpin during the lightweight clash at Dundrod in 1967. After Stuart Graham's challenge fizzled out when his works Suzuki developed plug trouble, Read shadowed the race leader all the way home. Ivy's Irish victory clinched the 125cc world title with Read finishing runner-up in the points table. The following year the gloves were most definitely off as far as Read was concerned. He defied team orders to end the season as 125cc and 250cc World Champion, an achievement that is still overshadowed by the acrimony that boiled between the Yamaha team mates long after the season ended.

Photo: Esler Crawford

50 John Blanchard (Seeley AJS), 62 Chris Conn (Norton), and 54 Ian McGregor (Norton) round Milburn Corner during the 1967 North West 200 350cc race. Fred Stevens was the hero of the day taking the win in both the 350cc and 500cc races, and giving the Hannah Paton marque its only success at Portstewart. On the day Conn was in contention for a podium place right to the end but lost out on third place to Len Ireland. McGregor's finest hour on the Triangle was his 350cc win in 1965. Blanchard claimed North West 200 wins in 1966 (250cc race) and 1969 (500cc).

Photo: Ralph Bryans Collection

Classic action from the 1968 Carrowdore 100 as Ray McCullough shadows Michael McGarrity (both Aermacchi) during their 350cc battle. McGarrity took the win by inches.

Photo: Clifford McLean

Nothing matched the sights and sounds of the Cookstown 100 when, for decades, on a Wednesday in early summer racing motor cycles would use the broad main street of the Co. Tyrone market town as a race track. The last time the Cookstown 100 was held on a Wednesday was in 1974. Since then the meeting has been held on a Saturday, usually at the beginning of the road racing season, and the race is now held on the short Orritor circuit that takes the action well away from the town.

This photo of the 1968 500cc race, run over the almost-7-mile Grange circuit includes: 9 B Hussey (496 Matchless), 1 Ian McGregor (Ryan Norton), 27 J L Telford (349 Nor-BSA), 24 Bertie Bradford (349 Norton), 30 J Johnston (496 Matchless), 5 Ken Kay (344 Aermacchi), 14 D J Houston (350cc Norton), 17 C R B Hutton (496 Matchless). Cecil Crawford took the 500cc win, whilst Brian Steenson scored a memorable 250cc/350cc double.

Photo: Derek McIntyre

TANDRAGEE "100"

MOTOR CYCLE ROAD RACE

PROMOTED BY NORTH ARMAGH MOTOR CYCLE AND CAR CLUB LTD.
(Affiliated to the Motor Cycle Union of Ireland Ulster Centre)

TANDRAGEE, CO. ARMAGH
SATURDAY, 3rd MAY, 1969

ROADS CLOSE	1.00 p.m.
PRACTICE	1.30 p.m.
START	2.00 p.m.

OFFICIAL PROGRAMME 2'6

Brian Steenson gets his head down on his Aermacchi as he tries to break clear from the chasing Honda of Bill Smith during the 350cc race at the 1968 North West 200. Steenson's efforts were in vain and he had to settle for the runner-up spot behind the much more experienced, Chester-based Smith.

Steenson's career was brief but brilliant. His first race was in 1966, and after attracting the support of Ronnie Conn and Mick Mooney and riding under the banner of Irish Racing Motorcycles, Steenson was soon making his mark as a world-class road racer. The year 1968 brought a 350cc third place at the 350cc Ulster Grand Prix behind Agostini and Carruthers. He went one better the following year at the Ulster with a stirring ride that electrified the home crowd after leading the 500cc race in the opening laps, before eventually being overhauled by race-winner Agostini. Steenson also followed the popular Italian home to claim runner-up spot in the '69 Junior TT. He had been placed as high as sixth in the '69 Senior (pictured below) before mechanical failure forced him out on the penultimate lap.

Steenson seemed poised on the brink of achieving great things in his chosen sport, when in June 1970, on the third lap of the Senior TT, whilst holding second place behind Agostini, Brian Steenson lost control of his Seeley and crashed heavily at the Mountain Box. He died from his injuries in Noble's Hospital. He was 23 years old.

Photo: Bertie Martin

Photo: Derek McIntyre

<<Opposite page

Saturday 9th August 1969, a moment in time frozen through the lens of ace lensman Derek McIntyre.

At first glance maybe there is nothing that remarkable about the shot. Another rider not readily identifiable at first glance, typical of the time, in pudding-basin helmet and plain black leathers, on a bike that looks every bit a home-made special, with little time or thought given to looks or presentation.

But take a closer look. See the hammer marks that pock-mark the fairing where it was fashioned roughly in someone's garage or shed? See the name on the side of the fairing? J Dunlop. Look at the long hair flying out the back of the pudding-basin helmet, at the unmistakable style. This is the man who, without a shadow of a doubt, was the greatest rider we ever had the privilege of watching, pictured at the very beginning of his career. Learning the basics on North Antrim's narrow country roads on a little 199cc Triumph just a few months past his seventeenth birthday. This is the earliest pure road racing photo of Joey Dunlop known to exist. It is a rare and important photo. There is one other taken in April 1969, but it is at Maghaberry short circuit, and the little Triumph is naked, rough and ready without a fairing. This shot shows that between April and August 1969, the young Dunlop had decided that a fairing was a necessity and had gone about making his own.

When we came across this photograph in Derek McIntyre's negative archive the first process was establishing that it was who we thought it was. The one element that didn't ring true was the leathers and the boots. They look too good, too new, for anything that Joey would usually have been seen in during the early days. And then we showed the photo to Davy Louden, married to Joey's sister Helen, and he told me without a moment's hesitation, that's definitely him. Davy had even loaned Joey the boots and leathers. The helmet belonged to Mervyn Robinson, his brother-in-law. It had been Robbo's first helmet.

Photo: Derek McIntyre

Scottish raider Roy Graham loaded his bikes on to the Irish Ferry line on countless occasions. More often than not the journey was well worth his while and Graham had added to his collection of silverware before making the return trip. The 1969 Mid Antrim 150 was no different. After leading the 500cc race in the early stages Graham slipped back to fourth before fighting past a quality field to claim second place behind Brian Steenson.

Pictured on the opening lap: 5 Graham (Matchless) leads from 2 Cecil Crawford (Norton), 1 Brian Steenson (Seeley), 6 Roy Reid (Norton), 3 Gerry Mateer (Norton) and 7 Len Ireland (Aermacchi).

Photo: Derek McIntyre

One of the last places you would expect to see a fully-fledged Grand Prix star riding exotic works machinery is on Tyrone's narrow country roads that comprise the course for the Cookstown 100, but that's exactly what was on offer at the 1969 Cookstown. The Cookstown was held that year on the Wednesday of the week following the North West 200. One of the star attractions at the North West 200 had been Czech star Franta Stastny, works Grand Prix rider for the Jawa factory. When the Cookstown had extended an invite to Stastny to ride at their smaller and less prestigious event, Stastny readily accepted and travelled to Cookstown with his single-cylinder, water-cooled 250cc Jawa, as well as a 350cc mount. Ballymoney's Derek McIntyre was on hand to capture the historic event and we have selected two of his shots here from that day.

(**Above**) Riding Number 34 Stastny on his way to fourth place on the 250cc Jawa, finishing behind Billy Guthrie, Tom Herron and Alfie Mayers; and (**right**) riding Number 50 competing in the 350cc race.

Photos: Derek McIntyre

1970s

In 1970 the organizers of the North West 200 opted to introduce a Production race for the first time. The new class attracted a quality entry contesting production-based races for 750cc, 500cc and 250cc machinery. Cliff Carr claimed his only North West 200 in the 250cc Production race, and in doing so gave the Spanish Ossa factory their only victory at the meeting. At the flag Carr held a lead of over a minute over the Suzuki-mounted Ralph Bryans. Pictured heading towards Henry Corner with every vantage point taken.

Photo: Clifford McLean

One of the most talented and charismatic riders to ever grace a race track, Italy's Giacomo Agostini exits Leathemstown on his way to victory on the 500cc MV Agusta during his last appearance at Dundrod in 1970. Ago remains the most successful rider of all time, amassing a total of 122 Grand Prix victories and fifteen world championship titles during his career. A firm favourite with the Irish fans Agostini raced at Dundrod from 1966 to 1970 and racked up seven wins at the circuit.

Photo: Clifford McLean

After years of trying, Jack Findlay took his first Grand Prix win at the 1971 Ulster. Pictured on the 500cc Suzuki on his way through the Windmill in style.

Photo: Derek McIntyre

This photograph captures a moment in history that elevated forever Irish favourite Ray McCullough to the status of living legend. He is the last Irish rider to win his home Grand Prix, the 1971 250cc race. McCullough's win had all the ingredients of a *Boy's Own* tale, and the hallmarks of greatness stamped all over it.

McCullough didn't travel well or far to pursue his racing career, but on Dundrod's wet and twisting roads on a rainy day in August 1971, the Dromara Destroyer proved that he was a match for the world's finest. In a textbook display of wet-weather riding, McCullough disappeared in a wall of spray to head a top three of Jarno Saarinen and Dieter Braun home. Pictured side by side with Saarinen in the opening miles of his epic ride at Leathemstown.

Photo: Derek McIntyre

The ground shakes beneath your feet as the assembled might of the 1971 Temple 100 combined 500cc and Unlimited Class thunder into action and set off on eight laps of the historic circuit. They are: 1 Gerry Mateer (Norton), 2 Denis Gallagher (354cc Yamsel), 3 Ray McCullough (498cc QUB Seeley), 4 Abe Alexander (496cc Seeley), 6 Bill McCosh (496cc Seeley), 8 Roy Graham (496cc Tickle Manx), 9 G Dowie (500cc Matchless), 10 Wilfie Herron (500cc Seeley), and 15 Sam McClements (499cc Norton).

Photo: Derek McIntyre

The 1970s weren't all *Star Wars*, punk rock and Barry Sheene. For some of us the golden days of our teenage years will be remembered for the ridiculous flares we thought we looked the "dog's bollocks" in, for the shirt collars so wide you were in serious danger of taking off in a stiff breeze, and for those permanent Bad Hair Days. Saturdays in the summer months were often spent fighting to find a hole in a hedge at places like the Temple 100 and Dundrod so we could get a glimpse of our racing heroes. And there were few who filled the title of hero better than Ray McCullough. Pictured on Temple's notorious jumps in 1971 with the crowd only feet from the action egging him on.

Photo: Derek McIntyre

Before she met Tom Herron and became his wife, Andrea Williams was an accomplished racer in her own right. But then when your family name is Williams, racing motor cycles has got to be in the blood. Andrea's brother is Peter Williams, a rider whose name is synonymous with the works Norton in the early 1970s, and her father Jack was an influential designer with AJS. This rare shot of Andrea Williams was taken of her at full cry on her 250cc Yamaha during her short-lived outing at the 1972 Mid Antrim 150. Her race was over before she had completed a lap, and her day ended with a broken collar bone and a trip to Ballymena's Waveney Hospital.

Photo: Derek McIntyre

Ian McGregor leads Tom Herron in their battle for supremacy during the 350cc race at the 1972 Mid Antrim 150. At the end of the 8-lapper it was Herron first past the flag with Billy Guthrie squeezing past McGregor to claim the runner-up spot.

Photo: Derek McIntyre

After fifteen years of racing on the Isle of Man, in 1973 Tommy Robb finally took the win he so richly deserved. Drafted in as a late replacement for the injured Chas Mortimer, Robb led the 125cc race from start to finish to take the win from Dutch challenger Jan Kostwinder.

The 250cc Production also provided a memorable TT moment for Robb when he took third place behind Charlie Williams and Eddie Roberts. Pictured on the 250cc Production Honda.

Photo: Derek McIntyre

The Dutch had Wil Hartog, known around the 1970s' Grands Prix paddocks as the White Giant because of his favoured colour of leathers. We had Abe Alexander and he more often than not did us proud. Pictured crossing the Brougshane Road and sweeping past Turtles Garage during the 1973 Mid Antrim 150.

Photo: Norman Waddell

Joey Dunlop's illustrious career began in 1969, and by 1973 Joey was beginning to come to the notice of fans and fellow competitors. The rising star was still learning his craft, riding this 344cc Aermacchi, but the Italian four-stroke was no match for the likes of the Yamahas, Yamsels and Suzukis that were the chosen mounts of the front men, Abe Alexander, Ray McCullough, Billy Guthrie and Tom Herron. In 1973 the long-haired country boy from Armoy was still rough around the edges. In the years ahead the whole world would learn his name.

Photo: Norman Waddell

Billy Guthrie's claimed his finest results at the Isle of Man TT with a brace of third-place finishes in the Junior and Senior TTs in 1976, and a Senior TT runner-up spot behind Tom Herron in 1978. Guthrie was a hugely popular figure on the Irish scene, and the highlight in a career littered with success came via a 500cc North West 200 win in 1973. Guthrie was associated with a wide variety of machinery during his racing years including AJS, Aermacchi, Greeves, and in the latter years a RG Suzuki. Billy Guthrie's death in 1995, the result of a sudden illness, was a major shock to the motor-cycling fraternity. Pictured here, Yamaha-mounted, tiptoeing home to a fine fifth place in the rain during the 1974 Formula 750 TT.

Photo: Norman Waddell

Tom Herron pushes away at the start of the 1974 Senior TT. The race was won by Phil Carpenter while Herron failed to make any impact on the Senior results, but overall the '74 TT was a resounding success for the Co. Down rider — Herron left The Island with a clutch of replicas after riding like a demon throughout the TT fortnight. His best result came in the Lightweight 125cc TT where he came home third in an all-Yamaha top three headed by Clive Horton and Ivan Hodgkinson, but Herron also had fourth-place finishes in the Junior and Lightweight 250cc races. Tom Herron went on to win a Senior and Lightweight TT double in 1976, and repeated his Senior TT success in 1978.

Photo: Norman Waddell

The very foundations of the wee house in the background on the coast road between Portrush and Portstewart groan under the weight of spectators as they watch John Williams on his way to a place in history. In 1974 he became the first man in the history of the North West 200 to score a hat trick of wins in one day when he won the 350cc, 500cc and 750cc races. We thought there was no one like him, and thousands of us were fully-paid-up members of the John G Williams fan club. His achievement on the Triangle circuit on that day in May 1974 was remarkable. It was a devastating blow when the quiet man from Cheshire died in hospital after crashing at Wheelers Corner during the 1978 Ulster Grand Prix.

Photo: Clifford McLean

OFFICIAL PROGRAMME **30p**

IRELAND'S NATIONAL NORTH-WEST '200'

SATURDAY, 19th MAY, 1973

Held under the General Competition Rules of the I.S.C. of the F.I.M. and G.C.R. of the M.C.U.I. and U.C.

105 Charlie Williams, complete with over-suit as some protection against the conditions, tiptoes through the damp patches on Blackhill during practice for the 1976 North West 200. Williams was quite simply one of the best riders of his generation, and as well as notching up a career total of eight TT victories between 1973 to 1980, he scored three North West 200 wins — the 350cc races in 1975 and 1980, and a 500cc victory in 1981.

Photo: Clifford McLean

Stan Woods marked his appearance at the 1976 Ulster Grand Prix with a famous 500cc victory and a third-place finish in the 1000cc race behind Geoff Barry and Tony Rutter. Joey Dunlop mounted a red-hot challenge for the 500cc honours, and in the heat of battle Woods earned the distinction of being the first rider to lap Dundrod in under four minutes when he posted a time of 111.30 mph. Pictured at the start of the 500cc race 41 Woods pushes the Suzuki into life alongside 11 Steve Tonkin, 2 Tony Rutter, 14 Martin Sharpe, 19 Geoff Barry, 8 Ian Richards, 34 R McKee, 10 Eddie Roberts and 1 Jackie Wilkin.

Photo: Clifford McLean

Joey Dunlop negotiates Ramsay Hairpin during his first visit to the Isle of Man TT Mountain circuit in 1976. It was by his standards a low key beginning with Dunlop taking sixteenth place in the Junior and eighteenth in the Senior races, but he wasn't there to win, he was there to learn. One story that is just one strand of the TT legend that continues to grow around Joey's TT achievements is that on his first lap of practice he was unfamiliar with the course and on arriving at Ballacraine had to wait for another rider to pass so he could follow him — by his own admission Dunlop was unsure whether the course went right or left at that point. In light of that it is all the more remarkable that Dunlop returned to the island only twelve months later to take his maiden win, the first of 26 TT victories that would take as many years to achieve. Simply the greatest road racer who ever lived.

Photo: Norman Waddell

Ron Haslam is already sitting up and ready to take evasive action as Geoff Barry's Yamaha begins to slide from under him at Tornagrough during the ill-fated Killinchy 150 in 1977. The accident claimed the life of the hugely-popular Barry who was a regular visitor to Ireland, taking on the best road racers on their home patch. On his day Geoff Barry was a match for anyone around.

Photo: Jim McBride

The frantic battle for the 250cc minor placings reaches Wheelers Corner during the 1977 Killinchy 150 with Billy Redmond leading the all-Yamaha trio of Ivor Greenwood and Davy Wood. Whilst Ray McCullough headed Joey Dunlop and Courtney Junk home to take the win, Redmond held onto fifth place for most of the race before slipping to seventh on the last lap.

Photo: Derek McIntyre

A **young Ron Haslam looks relaxed** and carefree as the sun shines over the North West 200 paddock in 1977. The legend on his van proclaims "Ron Haslam Superstar", a description that would prove prophetic in the years ahead as Haslam rose through the ranks, with spells as a factory rider with Honda and the distinctive Elf 500cc machine, to a place as a Grand Prix star. This is the partnership that first brought Haslam to the attention of the road-racing public, riding Mal Carter's distinctive and lightning-quick Pharoah Yamahas.

Photo: Derek McIntyre

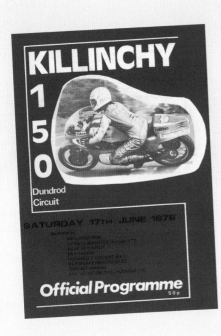

This is a sight you are unlikely ever to see again, some of the best road racers in the business airborne and wheel to wheel on Temple's notorious bumps and jumps. Unlike nowadays the crowds were allowed to stand where they liked to a large extent, and the action was rarely anything less than electrifying. This epic picture, taken during the 1978 Temple 100 by Derek McIntyre, shows Courtney Junk and Adrian Craig in the thick of the action.

Photo: Derek McIntyre

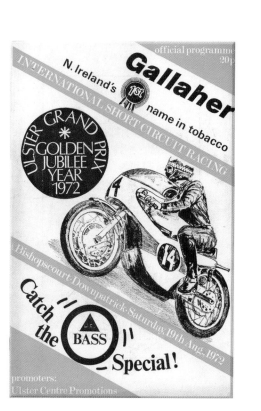

The venue is the Temple's famous jumps in 1978 again, and this time the camera was in the hands of Jim McBride as he captures Joey Dunlop and Noel Hudson in mid-flight. All that is good about Irish road racing is here — the sun shining down as our home-grown superstars push their machinery to the limits on Ulster's country roads, with the fans only feet from the action.

Photo: Jim McBride

Tom Herron's storming performance in front of his devoted fans at the 1978 Ulster Grand Prix remains a fitting epitaph to the memory of the home-grown hero who was one of the finest riders to leave these shores, and who was at the time a road racer at the peak of his powers. On the day Herron scored a classy treble of victories comprising wins in the TT Formula 1 and 1000cc races, as well as this flag-to-flag 250cc win ahead of Jon Ekorold and Trevor Steele. Pictured down on the tank as he flashes through the Quarry Bends.

Photo: Clifford McLean

Ray McCullough cresting Quarry Hill, flat out and inches from the crowd during the 1978 North West 200. McCullough's distinguished career began riding a 196cc Triumph Tiger Cub at the 1960 Tandragee 100. His début ride ended in mechanical failure, but McCullough continued racing, appearing on a wide mix of machinery including Greeves, Norton, Bultaco, Harley Davidson, and the Queens University Yamsels and Yamahas. In 1970 McCullough began racing under the Irish Racing Motorcycle's banner of sponsor Mick Mooney. It was a partnership that would endure for fourteen years until McCullough's retirement in 1984 from the sport he graced for almost a quarter of a century.

His career highlights are too many to list, but some of the most memorable included a famous 250cc win in the rain at Oulton Park over Barry Sheene in 1971, his now-legendary 250cc Ulster Grand Prix victory (again in the rain) in 1971, the first of a total of seven Ulster Grand Prix wins, and the only dead heat (shared with Tony Rutter) in the 1977 350cc North West 200. McCullough was safe, brave and very, very fast. He did it all with a smile on his face and with the help of his loyal friend and mechanic Hubert Gibson.

Photo: Jim McBride

By 1979 Tom Herron's sheer class whilst still ranked as a privateer as demonstrated on the Grands Prix circuits of the world had finally earned Herron a berth alongside Barry Sheene in the world championship Heron Suzuki team. It seemed there was no limit to what Herron might achieve, and the results from the early Grands Prix of the 1979 season seemed to bear out the opinion of those who believed that Herron could go the whole way in his challenge for a world title. Then everything changed. Herron crashed at the Spanish Grand Prix held at Jarama, and it seemed that his participation in the North West 200 was unlikely due to the injuries he had sustained. However, despite all of that Herron took his place on the grid at Portstewart a week later. It was another step in a chain of events that combined to mark the 1979 North West 200 as the worst day in the history of the event. A series of high-speed crashes throughout the day claimed the lives of young Scottish visitor Brian Hamilton, and of local Armoy Armada hero Frank Kennedy, and then on the final corner of the last lap of the last race of the day Herron lost control of his Suzuki at Juniper Hill. The injuries he sustained were too much for even Herron to overcome. He died in Coleraine Hospital that evening. Pictured during the fateful 1979 North West 200 at Shell Hill Bridge.

Photo: Norman Waddell

1980s

SUPPORTERS CLUB 1989 UGP

In 1980 the Formula One world championship was contested over two rounds, the Isle of Man TT and the Ulster Grand Prix. Joey didn't contest the Isle of Man round but was drafted into the works Suzuki team to ride shotgun for Kiwi title-contender Graeme Crosby. He did what he was asked to do — and finished behind Crosby and ahead of the Honda of Mick Grant. Crosby won the title by two points from Grant, whilst Dunlop's solitary outing was enough to seal third place in the championship. Crosby retained the title in 1981 whilst Joey finished third once again. Pictured rounding Leathemstown with Rob McIlnea (750cc Yamaha) in tow.

Photo: Norman Waddell

Popular English raider Pete Wild ended up runner-up in the 250cc North West 200 races two years on the trot in 1981 and 1982. Wild followed Steve Tonkin home in 1981 and was once again the nearly-man the following year, losing out to Donny Robinson despite sharing the fastest lap of the race with Robinson and Con Law. Pictured at Metropole Corner in 1981.

Photo: Clifford McLean

This photograph sums up the scenes and atmosphere that made the Carrowdore 100 unique for so many years. The crowds spill out of the pubs to line the main street and look on as Joey Dunlop chases Michael McGarrity during their torrid encounter in the 1983 125cc race. Both had turns at the front, but as the advantage seesawed between them, it was Robert Dunlop who took the race by the scruff of the neck and stayed out in front to the flag. Joey settled for third spot behind McGarrity in the end.

Photo: Derek McIntyre

Someone once said that if road racing was invented today it would be banned by tea time! This photograph of the start of the 1983 350cc Carrowdore 100 shows a sight you'll never see again, the main street of an Irish town filled with racing machinery as the howl of engines rends the air, and the crowd pack the footpaths up to the edges of the road. It's a sight that would make the head of any Health and Safety Executive Officer spin.

Leading them away is 5 Johnny Rea, 1 Brian Reid, 3 Courtney Junk, 2 Con Law, 4 Noel Hudson, 6 Gerry Brennan, 18 Davy Cowan, 8 Ray McCullough, 10 Denis Todd, 17 Martin Barr, 22 Trevor Steele and 21 J Knox.

Photo: Derek McIntyre

ROAD AND CIRCUIT '82-83
AN ANDERSON TEAM RACING ENTERPRISE £1

★ FIXTURES   ★ RESULTS   ★ REVIEWS
★ QUIZZES   ★ PHOTOGRAPHS
★ INFORMATION

Joey refuels during this hectic pit stop at the final round of the Formula 1 world championship at Zolder, Belgium in 1984. After the previous round at Dundrod ended in controversy, Dunlop travelled to Belgium expecting nothing less than a showdown for the title with his Honda team mate Roger Marshall. The anticipated head-to-head never materialized after Marshall was forced out of the race with a blown head gasket. Dunlop received a hero's welcome when he returned home with his third world championship secured.

Photo: Unknown

Norman Brown rounds York Corner during the 1983 North West 200. An Isle of Man Senior TT victory in 1982 was arguably the highlight of Brown's career. He scored a memorable hat trick at Skerries later the same year and the Newry man added a 350cc North West 200 win to his CV in 1983. Tragically Norman Brown lost his life in a freak accident at Silverstone during the British Grand Prix in 1983.

Photo: Derek McIntyre

The all-Suzuki battle between Denis Ireland and Steve Henshaw crests Juniper Hill during the 1985 North West 200 Superbike race. All that is good about pure road racing can be seen here: out and out speed, glorious weather, some of the best in the business going wheel to wheel, and the crowd packed like sardines and close enough to breathe down the riders' necks.

Photo: Derek McIntyre

Joey Dunlop kick-starts the defence of his Formula 1 crown on the RVF 750cc Honda at Hockenheim, May 1986. The '86 campaign had faltered from the off when Dunlop ran out of fuel on the final lap of the opening round at Misano. Joey derived some consolation from setting the fastest lap of the race, but returned to Ballymoney with zero points as opposed to home winner Marco Lucchinelli's maximum.

Joey set about putting things right with a storming ride to victory at Hockenheim. In the end there was nothing to worry about. Dunlop claimed the top step on the podium in four of the six remaining rounds as well as the runner-up spot at Dundrod behind a charging Neil Robinson.

Photo: Derek McIntyre

Joey Dunlop digs deep and fights against the pain during the 1986 Formula 1 world championship round at Jerez. Not only did Dunlop have the heat and the opposition to contend with, he also carried injuries including broken ribs, sustained during a car crash after a late-night celebratory lap of Assen two weeks earlier went wrong. Dunlop, Neil "Smutty" Robinson and Derek McIntyre (the photographer who took this picture) were amongst a seven-strong contingent returning from the prize-giving night out, when mechanic Dave Sleat lost control of their car whilst attempting to lap the Dutch circuit. The vehicle overturned and the night out ended in the local casualty department. Despite finishing in fifth place at Jerez Dunlop was in mighty form for the rest of the season and retained his title with over 30 points to spare over nearest challenger Paul Iddon.

Photo: Derek McIntyre

Despite the fairing on the left side of his Skoal Bandit Suzuki coming adrift at the worst possible time, Neil "Smutty" Robinson remains at full cry through the streets of Villa Real during the Portuguese round of the 1986 Formula 1 world championship. The race win went to Joey Dunlop who dominated for the entire distance. Robinson had ridden superbly to keep his challenge alive in the early stages, but lost over two minutes in the pits to allow running repairs when his fairing worked loose. He rejoined the fray to eventually finish in fifth place. It was a continuation of the bad luck that had ended his race whilst leading the Dutch round at Assen earlier in the year. The Formula 1 win he so richly deserved came in August in front of his home crowd at Dundrod when he scored an emphatic victory over the world champion. And then, when it seemed that Neil Robinson had the world at his feet, fate struck the cruellest blow. Less than a month after his famous Ulster Grand Prix victory Neil Robinson lost his life after crashing at Olivers Mount, Scarborough.

Photo: Derek McIntyre

Joey Dunlop receives the applause of the crowd after an emphatic win on the sweltering streets of Villa Real, Portugal, Formula 1 world championship, 20th July 1986.

Photo: Derek McIntyre

The mighty Rothmans Hondas of Roger Marshall and Joey Dunlop nip through Juniper Chicane during North West 200 practice in 1986. The meeting would end for the second year running with honours even and the score standing at one Superbike race win each. The rivalry was always intense between the two, and at times, such as their epic Formula I race at Dundrod in 1984, nearly boiled over.

Photo: Alastair McCook

40th ANNIVERSARY OF THE
MID ANTRIM '150'
NATIONAL ROAD RACE
RATHKENNY CIRCUIT BALLYMENA
SATURDAY 23rd AUGUST 1986
Roads Close 12.00 Noon   Starts 1.00 P.M.

ORGANISED BY
THE MID ANTRIM MOTOR CLUB LTD.
(Senior Motor Cycle Section)

OFFICIAL PROGRAMME £2.00

Roger Burnett flicks the Rothmans Honda through Juniper Chicane during practice for the 1986 North West 200. Burnett didn't feature in the 1986 North West 200 results, but a month later caused a major upset by winning the Senior TT in style. Whilst Burnett's Honda team mates Roger Marshall and Joey Dunlop were plagued with mechanical problems that saw them struggle home well outside the top three, Burnett's 3-cylinder two-stroke never missed a beat as he led Geoff Johnston and Barry Woodland home.

Photo: Alastair McCook

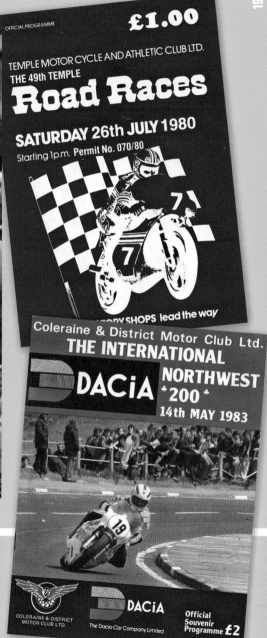

Steve Cull parks the 350cc Yamaha on the footpath at Metropole Corner during practice for the 1986 North West 200. One of the most popular riders of his generation Cull amassed a total of six North West 200 wins between 1980 and 1988, including a famous hat trick at the 1988 meeting.

Photo: Alastair McCook

Eddie Laycock pictured in action at the Fore road races in 1986. Laycock was a prime example of the rare breed of rider who produces fireworks as easily on a purpose-built track as on a pure road circuit. During his distinguished career Eddie Laycock competed as a 500cc Grand Prix rider, riding for the Joe Millar team from 1989 until his retirement in 1992. His best season came in 1991 when he finished in twelfth place in the 500cc points table.

As a road racer Laycock was as good as it got, claiming two Isle of Man TT victories, the 1987 Junior and the 1989 Supersport 400cc. Laycock recorded four 250cc Class wins at the North West 200, in 1986, 1987 and a classy double in 1990 after a big off in practice at Blackhill. The popular Dubliner amassed five Ulster Grand Prix victories between 1986 and 1989.

Eddie Laycock retired from racing in 1992 and now works as a commentator on RTE television's coverage of Moto GP.

Photo: Norman Waddell

Joey Dunlop gets the Bol D'Or-winning Honda off the line at the start of the last round of the 1987 Formula I world championship at Donington Park. Heading him off the line is the Bimota of Davide Tardozzi (3) and the Bimota-Yamaha of Peter Rubatto (2). Dunlop needed a miracle to retain his title, and it didn't arrive. Whilst Joey took third place, a 7th-place finish was enough for Virginio Ferrari to steal the Formula I crown away from Ballymoney for the first time in five years. Thousands of Irish fans believed Dunlop's crown was merely on loan. It was the end of an era.

Photo: Derek McIntyre

Steve Hislop, one of the most naturally-talented riders to grace a race track, puts the works Honda through its paces at Metropole Corner during the 1989 North West 200. Hislop scored a classy 750cc/Superbike double, and but for Brian Reid's heroics would have added the 600cc race win as well. Other highlights of Hislop's '89 season also included an electrifying TT Formula 1 win over Carl Fogarty at Dundrod, and a classy Supersport 600/TT Formula 1/Senior treble in the Isle of Man. Simply a genius.

Photo: Clifford McLean

Kawasaki

COCA COLA
International
16th May
North West 200
(Roads close 11am)
Practice Days 12th & 14th May
Roads closed 30pm

COLERAINE & DISTRICT MOTOR CLUB LTD. AUTHORISES:

.... TO ACT IN THE CAPACITY OF:—
Signed B. NUTT Clerk of Course.

PRESS

1990s

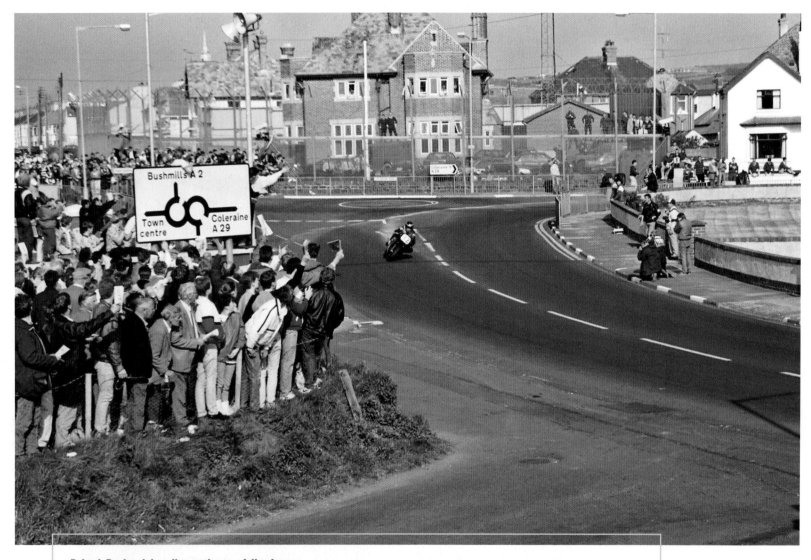

Robert Dunlop takes the applause of the fans as he rounds Metropole Corner on the final lap of the 1990 North West 200 Superbike race. The race win, including a new absolute course record of 121.04 mph, completed a hat trick for the diminutive star, and gave Norton their first victory on the Triangle since Dick Creith won the 1965 500cc race. (Note the RUC officers, in the background, standing on the roofs of police Land-Rovers® for a better view.)

Photo: Alastair McCook

Brian Reid launches the 600cc Budweiser Yamaha on Carrowdore's flat-out jumps during the 1991 meeting. As a road racer Reid was peerless. Undoubtedly the crowning achievement of a career littered with success was his back-to-back Formula 2 world titles won in 1985 and '86. A staunch supporter of the TT Reid took his first podium finish in the 1984 Junior TT, and went on to rack up a total of five wins on the Mountain circuit including a classy 400cc Supersport/Junior double at the 1992 TT. Between 1983 and 1992 Reid took eight wins at the Ulster Grand Prix, including doubles in 1983 and 1992. His only North West 200 win came in the 1989 600cc race. Brian Reid's career ended after a serious accident at the Temple 100 in 1994.

Photo: Clifford McLean

Two legends of Irish road racing, Joey Dunlop and Phillip McCallan, round Clough Hairpin together during the 1991 Mid Antrim 150. McCallan was often cast in the role of Young Pretender as he regularly challenged Dunlop's supremacy as King of the Roads. When the chips were down McCallan never underestimated or lacked respect for his great rival, but he pushed him harder than most dared.

Photo: Alastair McCook

All eyes are on Alan Irwin as he guns the McAdoo Honda underneath the railway bridge and on towards Portstewart during the 1992 North West 200 Superbike race. Irwin remains the most successful Irish rider of all time in terms of total number of career race wins. The victory on the big occasion always eluded him though he often came close. In '92 he made it onto the podium with a fighting 250cc third-place finish. Possibly his best day at the North West 200 came in 1987 when he finished runner-up behind Joey Dunlop in both Superbike races.

Photo: Alastair McCook

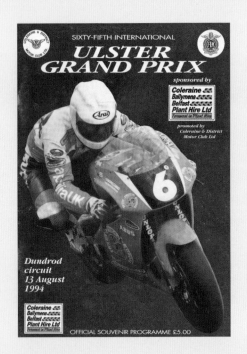

Stephen Farmer makes the little 125cc Honda sing as he flashes through Dhu Varren during the 1992 North West 200. Farmer was one of Ireland's most promising racing prospects for years but sadly was cruelly robbed of the chance to fulfil his true potential. In a bitter double blow to the Farmer family Stephen Farmer lost his life in a non-racing related accident — his cousin Mark died only months earlier after crashing on the New-Zealand-built Britten during practice for the 1994 TT.

Photo: Alastair McCook

Isle of Man '93
T
31 May - 11 June
Road Racing Capital of the World

Phillip McCallan rounds Quarter Bridge on the works RC30 Honda en route to victory in the 1993 Senior Isle of Man TT. McCallan's style was spectacular, all knees and elbows, but very effective. This win brought his TT tally to three. In the years ahead he broke the hearts of the opposition over and over again as he chalked up a total of eleven TT victories, including 38 120+-mph laps on the Mountain circuit.

Photos: Alastair McCook

Robert Dunlop leads his brother Joey and Brian Reid out of Creg-Ny-Baa and on towards Brandish Corner during their epic battle for honours in the 1993 Junior TT. Whilst mechanical problems forced Robert out of the race, Reid produced a storming ride to take his fifth and final TT victory by seven seconds from Jim Moodie, with Joey Dunlop completing the podium.

Photo: Alastair McCook

In 1993 Joey Dunlop achieved what many said would never be done, he surpassed TT legend Mike Hailwood's record of fourteen Isle of Man wins. Dunlop's hard-fought 125cc victory in 1993 gave him one more win than Hailwood, an achievement that set the racing world alight. Most other sporting superstars would have opted for a champagne celebration. Not Joey, he was quite happy to sit in the sunshine behind the beer tent and have a vodka and coke with his mates. Included in the photograph are (left) James Courtney (with arm in a cast), Ernie Coates (red shirt) and Denis McCullough (no shirt).

Photo: Alastair McCook

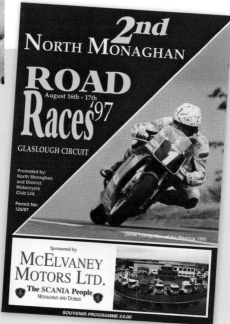

This is a photograph of Robert Dunlop at the very peak of his career, on the Medd RC45 Honda on Blackhill during practice for the 1994 North West 200. Dunlop went on to score his third hat trick at the event, and in the process claimed the first International win for Honda's new, troublesome Superbike. Weeks later Dunlop's world was in ruins after the rear wheel of the Honda disintegrated during the 1994 Formula 1 TT. The injuries Dunlop sustained that day finished him as Superbike rider. It would have spelt the end of racing for any other mere mortal. But then again Robert Dunlop isn't just any mere mortal. It is a fitting testimony to his sheer guts, bravery and determination that he not only raced again but won at the highest level, including an emotional 125cc TT win in 1998 on the circuit that very nearly claimed his life. It would be a foolish man who would bet against Robert Dunlop adding at least one more big win to his already impressive CV.

Photo: Alastair McCook

The grid lines up for the 1994 Dundrod 150 Open race, with the front row comprising from left to right Alan Irwin, Joey Dunlop, Brian Reid and nearest the camera Johnny Rea. Behind them on the second row of the grid is Gary Dynes (7). Brian Reid ended the day as the only rider from the front row without a race win, although he did finish in second place in the 250cc race. Rea and Irwin claimed a win apiece whilst Joey took the 250cc and 125cc wins.

Photo: Alastair McCook

The grid for the 1995 Mid Antrim 150 Support Race line up under the shadow of Clough village church. It's an image that demonstrates how in Irish road racing the everyday is transformed into an integral part of a high-speed circuit that may not have the sophistication or pizzazz of Monza or Daytona, but has a unique atmosphere that is unmatched anywhere.

Photo: Alastair McCook

Bob Jackson leads a young Darran Lindsay over Alexanders Jump during the 1995 Mid Antrim 150. Not an inch of rubber on the road and the pair of Hondas are hitting well over 120 mph and accelerating. Total focus, total concentration, and total trust in your fellow competitor.

Photo: Alastair McCook

MID~ANTRIM '150'

NATIONAL ROAD RACE 1992

Organised by
THE MID-ANTRIM CLUB LTD. MOTOR CYCLE SECTION

Joey Dunlop (600cc Harris Honda)
Photo by Roy Harris

CLOUGH CIRCUIT, BALLYMENA
SATURDAY 8th AUGUST, 1992

Official Programme
£3.00

A sight the opposition became well used to during the 1990s, Phillip McCallan first past the chequered flag. On this occasion Supermac is in the process of claiming the 600cc win at the 1995 North West 200, a race he led from start to finish, and won with ease from Mike Edwards and Bob Jackson.

Photo: Alastair McCook

This used to be the most spectacular place to take photographs in all of Irish road racing. On the road rising out of Carrowdore village where at times the bike flew so high and so far that you couldn't help thinking that it wasn't so much racing licences but pilots' licences they needed. In this shot of a particularly torrid 600cc encounter in 1996, Alan Irwin has just mono-wheeled out of the frame chased by Ricky Mitchell and Derek Young. Young's front wheel is way out of shape and when it came down he swept to the left bringing Derek and his Cladding Contracts Honda just that wee bit too close to the photographer for comfort. It's a photograph you don't have the opportunity to attempt anymore – the Carrowdore 100 hasn't been held since 2000, more's the pity.

Photo: Alastair McCook

McCullough, Dunlop and Dynes keep their 250cc Hondas absolutely nailed as they negotiate Carrowdore's flat-out jump during the 1997 meeting. Nothing you will see in road racing will inspire you and put the fear of God in you more than the sight of a clutch of screaming two-strokes, passing airborne, inches from your nose, on a September afternoon on Carrowdore's main street.

Photo: Alastair McCook

If there was any justice in the world Michael Rutter would have ended the 1996 North West 200 with a brace of Superbike wins to his credit — at least. Instead Rutter had to endure the agony of having both Superbike races seemingly in the bag, a huge lead in hand in both races, and then his McCullough Ducati quit, twice. Pictured at full cry heading towards Primrose Hill.

Photo: Alastair McCook

With everything tucked in behind the screens and fairings Denis McCullough and Owen McNally rip it up on their little 125cc Hondas through Armagh's winding country roads in this epic clash of the Tiddlers during the 1996 Tandragee 100. As usual the crowd are only feet from the action.

Photo: Alastair McCook

Chris Richardson, Derek Young, Richard Britton, Alan Irwin, Stephen Ferguson and Adrian Archibald duke it out in the 600cc race at the 1996 Tandragee 100. This corner is radically different nowadays, and is the site of a controversial man-made chicane, deemed unsafe by some and unpopular with most of those who race. In the days before the chicane this was the beginning of a fast right-hand sweep past the paddock gate. Now it's a fiddly right-left-right kink that is just waiting to trip up the unwary.

Photo: Alastair McCook

Johnny Rea, father of modern-day British Superbike star Jonathan, turns on the style at Tandragee in 1996. Johnny Rea was a formidable force in Irish racing, and ensured that every Regal 600cc race he competed in was a nail-biter to the end. Rea won at virtually every track in Ireland, and crowned his racing career with a famous Junior TT victory in 1989.

Photo: Alastair McCook

Simon Beck and Bob Jackson go head to head through Quarry Bends during the 1996 Ulster Grand Prix. The pair ended the day with a Superbike race runner-up finish each, and Jackson took the win in the 250c Classic race, but the day belonged to Phillip McCallan who made history by winning four races on the day.

Photo: Alastair McCook

NORTH MONAGHAN
& DISTRICT
MOTORCYCLE CLUB
LTD.

PRESS

With rain threatening, Chris Richardson peers over the top edge of his screen as he tries everything to keep Joey Dunlop at bay during the 1997 Ulster Grand Prix 125cc race at the frighteningly-fast Budore. When the rain eventually came Richardson could not match Dunlop's canny prowess on wet roads and settled for third place, behind Dunlop and Phelim Owens.

Photo: Alastair McCook

Held in April each year the Cookstown 100 is traditionally the first race on the Irish road racing calendar. The 1998 Cookstown 100, run over the 6.1-mile Skerrygroom circuit, posed major problems for riders and race organizers alike, when the newly resurfaced road circuit began to break up. As a result the racing line was strewn with loose stones which became deadly missiles when they were thrown up by bikes once racing was underway. The result was near-mayhem, with some riders suffering bruising and ending up with hefty repair bills for damage caused to their machines. This shot of racing veteran Paul Cranston sums it up. The screen on his 750cc Kawasaki looks like it has been peppered with shotgun pellets.

The following year the Cookstown 100 was moved to the Orritor circuit.

Photo: Alastair McCook

After missing the 1997 North West 200 Superbike race warm-up lap, Phillip McCallan was forced to start from the pit lane on cold tyres. Despite the "minor" setback McCallan almost achieved the impossible coming from dead last to claim fifth place at the end of the race. Pictured in determined mood as he tips into the start/finish chicane ahead of the 500cc V-Twin Honda of Woolsey Coulter.

Photo: Alastair McCook

600cc competitor Stevie Nugent in big trouble on Alexanders Jump during the 1997 Mid Antrim 150. Nugent was lucky and stayed on, thanks to skill, good judgment and a minor miracle.

Photo: Alastair McCook

Phelim Owens powers to victory in the 1997 Carrowdore 100 125cc race. Owens was a tenacious competitor, especially on 125cc machinery. He won the 125cc race at the North West 200 in 1995 and 1997, and between 1996 and 1999 Owens won the 125cc Ulster Grand Prix three times out of four, and settled for the runner-up spot behind Robert Dunlop in 1998.

Photo: Alastair McCook

Denis McCullough, nephew of Irish legend Ray McCullough, gets ready to race at Killalane in 1998. Denis McCullough was a stalwart of 125cc and 250cc racing, and more often than not could be seen locked in combat with his arch-rival and friend Gary Dynes. McCullough retired from the sport after being seriously injured in a racing accident that claimed the lives of Gary Dynes and Andy McLean at Glaslough, Co. Monaghan in 2000.

Photo: Alastair McCook

Robert Dunlop defies the limits of the human body as he powers Patsy O'Kane's 125cc Honda through Hillberry on his way to victory in the 1998 Isle of Man Ultra Lightweight TT. Dunlop's fight back from injuries sustained after crashing during the 1994 Formula 1 TT is well documented, as are the legal battles against officialdom that also threatened to halt Dunlop's long journey on the comeback trail. On top of that Robert sustained a broken collar bone and a broken ankle after crashing out of the 125cc race at the North West 200 two weeks earlier. That's what winners are made off: hard as nails with no soft centre.

Photo: Alastair McCook

Neat, stylish and always fast. Bob Jackson skims through Cochranestown during his rampage through the 1998 Dundrod 150 race card. Jackson took four wins — 250cc/Open, Regal 600cc, 500cc Classic and Senior races. He also set a new lap record in the Senior race of 123.66 mph to boot. A hugely talented and experienced competitor, Cumbrian Jackson became a virtually permanent fixture around the Irish racing scene over the years. Equally at home on Classic bikes as on the modern-day machinery Jackson notched up three Classic 250cc wins at the Ulster Grand Prix all Suzuki-mounted, as well as a Supersport 600cc win in 1997. Jackson also took the 250cc race win at the 1979 North West 200. But for a jammed fuel cap which seemed to take an eternity to free during his botched pit stop Bob Jackson should have won the 1998 Senior TT. Bob Jackson's racing career ended when he sustained serious back injuries after crashing during practice for the 1998 Mid Antrim 150.

Photo: Alastair McCook

Owen McNally is surrounded by family as the 125cc and 250cc machines are readied in the paddock on race morning, Ulster Grand Prix 1997. Whilst Owen's brother James (in overalls) helps out, his Uncle Danny looks on. It was a good day for the popular Coleraine rider who took his second International win of the season, adding a 250cc win to his 250cc North West 200 victory from earlier in the year.

Photo: Alastair McCook

Owen McNally wrestles the 250cc Bob Mullan Motors Honda past Paddock Corner and on to a runner-up finish at the 1998 Tandragee 100. McNally's ability on two-stroke racing machinery was exceptional, and his performance at the 1998 Tandragee 100 was crowned with a 125cc victory. The day was overshadowed by Joey Dunlop's big crash in the 125cc race. Joey may have ended the day battered and bruised, but it made little difference — in a matter of weeks he was back on the Isle of Man and winning again.

Photo: Alastair McCook

This was probably my favourite place for photographing road racing. The jump coming out of Carrowdore village had to be seen to be believed, the speed and sheer distance the bikes travelled in the air almost defied the laws of physics. The 1998 meeting provided this image of Denis McCullough and Owen McNally landing side by side at something around 140 mph. Behind them and almost obscured is Adrian Archibald. Simply breathtaking.

Photo: Alastair McCook

James Courtney prepares for a two-wheel landing on his 600cc Honda during the 1998 Temple 100. Many believed Courtney was the natural successor to Joey Dunlop as Ireland's Number 1 road racer. Courtney had bags of talent but at times if it hadn't been for bad luck he would have had no luck at all. The string of TT and International wins that were predicted never came to be, and James Courtney retired from racing in 2000 after a series of big crashes and serious injuries.

Photo: Alastair McCook

Andy McLean flies high and wide on Temple's notorious jumps on his beloved 250cc Yamaha. The Temple 100 was a regular feature of the Irish racing calendar until 2000. It was at once spectacular and very dangerous, and riders like Andy loved the challenge and thrill of the gruelling series of jumps on the treacherous Saintfield circuit. Tragically Andy McLean was fatally injured in an accident that also claimed the life of Gary Dynes at the North Monaghan road races, Glaslough, in 2000.

Photo: Ben McCook

The 600cc Regal machines of Richard Britton and Bob Jackson seem to hang in mid-air as they fly over the Temple 100's notorious jumps in 1998. Bringing up the rear and preparing for take-off are John Donnan and Adrian Archibald.

Photo: Alastair McCook

Stewart Parkhill just about stays in front of the Sanyo 250cc Honda of Denis McCullough as they sweep beneath the outstretched sycamore branches during the 1998 Killalane meeting. The Killalane course overlaps the Skerries 100 circuit in North Co. Dublin, and its traditional date in late September usually brings the road racing season to a fitting climax. If you could bottle the atmosphere at places like Skerries and Killalane you'd be a millionaire in no time.

Photo: Alastair McCook

The best 125cc road racers in the country go head to head during the 1998 North Monaghan road races at Glaslough. Dunlop, McNally, McCullough and Dynes scratching on the black stuff between the hedges.

Photo: Alastair McCook

Sometimes in the paddock before a race you saw a really intriguing, enigmatic side of Joey Dunlop that attracted you as a photographer as much as the style and bravery that appeared through the lens when he was on a race track. This time, Easter Saturday 1999 at Aghadowey, was such an occasion. At times before a race, even in the middle of a crowd, he was totally in a world of his own, 100% focused on the job in hand.

Photo: Alastair McCook

This photograph was taken during practice for the 600cc class at the Ulster Grand Prix in 1999 at the top of Tullyrusk, just before the crest of the Deers Leap. Adrian Archibald leads Joey Dunlop and Owen McNally in a wheel-to-wheel train at over 150 mph. To witness such a spectacle is truly stunning and frightening at the same time. In a matter of seconds from when they appear as dots in the distance at Leathemstown Crossroads, they're past you in a blur of colour and a howl of tortured metal. It's then you realize that you need to breathe, and like the dozens of times when you've stood here before and watched, you wonder how the hell they do what you just saw them do but didn't believe was possible.

Photo: Alastair McCook

This is how close the fans get to the action. The fans are an integral part of road racing — devoted, obsessed and fiercely loyal, travelling the length and breadth of the country, making the annual pilgrimage to the Isle of Man, following their sport and supporting the riders. This is the battle for the minor placings in the 125cc race at the Cookstown 100 in 1999. Last-minute entry Darran Lindsay is doing his best to show Nigel Moore a clean pair of heels. Moore, having his first 125cc ride on closed public roads, proved to be more than a handful for the more experienced Lindsay, and caught and passed him to finish runner-up to Owen McNally. Not that he needs any more encouragement but the Nigel Moore fans in the crowd offer it anyway.

Photo: Alastair McCook

Joey Dunlop looking neat and stylish as he lands his 250cc Honda on the notorious jump at Black's Farm on the Cookstown 100 Orritor circuit, April 1999.

Photo: Alastair McCook

Phillip McCallan's career finally came to an end in 1999. These three photographs show Supermac in action in the last three road races he contested during the '99 season. McCallan was forced to retire during the Isle of Man TT 1999, the cumulative result of serious injuries he suffered over his racing career. In the end the human body can only take so much, and despite McCallan being one of the most determined and focused individuals in racing, even he reached a stage where enough was enough. These photos were taken at the only three races he contested in 1999 — the final three races of Phillip's career.

A pensive Phillip McCallan on the grid for the Tandragee 100 in 1999. The Tandragee is McCallan's local race and the effect of his presence at the meeting electrified the home crowd. As it turned out it provided Phillip McCallan with the last victory of his career when he galloped his R1 Yamaha to first place in the final race of the meeting, the Senior. It could have been a double for Supermac but for the fact that he ran wide at Bells Crossroads when leading the Lambert & Butler/250cc race whilst in the lead. The mistake relegated McCallan to second place behind James Courtney.

Photo: Alastair McCook

Jim Moodie, Iain Duffus, Ian Lougher and James Courtney swarm behind Phillip McCallan as he tries everything he knows to keep out of reach on Mill Road, Portstewart, during the opening Superbike race at the 1999 North West 200. McCallan's final North West 200 yielded a 600cc runner-up spot, and third place in the final Superbike race of the meeting. McCallan later described it as "the ride from hell". He felt, as always, that he should have won. He nearly did, but only after receiving pain-killing injections in his injured shoulder on the grid.

Photo: Alastair McCook

Supermac at full cry through Kates Cottage during the 1999 Junior TT. Physically McCallan was far from fit, and fought through the pain barrier to claim seventh place in the Junior, a placing that fell short of his own high standards. His best result of the week came in the Production race where McCallan took the final place on the rostrum behind David Jeffries and Jason Griffiths. It would prove to be his last race, and it had taken guts and determination to compete at all. But the four gruelling laps over the Mountain circuit were the final straw. By then the pain in his injured shoulder became too much to ignore and, with his Yamaha R1 warmed, on the grid and ready for the 6-lap Senior TT, Phillip McCallan had no option but to turn his back and walk away. It was truly the end of an era, and the final act in the career of a rider who can justifiably be described as a legend.

Photo: Alastair McCook

This is a sight that Irish racing fans became well used to over the years, Denis McCullough and Gary Dynes armed with 250cc machinery and going head to head. I've lost count of the number of times you couldn't take a photograph of one without the other being in it. Here McCullough has the upper hand as they flick through Dukes Bends during the 250cc race at the Skerries 100 meeting. At the flag the positions were reversed and Dynes snuck past to claim the win.

Photo: Alastair McCook

Darran Lindsay leads Gary Dynes through Kepple Gate during the 1999 Ultra Lightweight TT. Dynes had suffered the earlier disappointment of being robbed of a podium finish in the Lightweight TT when engine problems dropped him to sixth place on the last lap when third place at least seemed guaranteed. There was no mistake on this occasion, and Dynes claimed the final place on the podium ahead of Lindsay and behind Lougher and McNally. The race was not without incident for Dynes who had a near-miss when Noel Clegg crashed out right in front of him at Greeba Castle, and had then the daunting task of continuing after having fuel accidentally splashed into his eyes during his fuel stop.

Photo: Alastair McCook

1 9 9 0 s

Despite recording his fastest ever TT lap of 123.06 mph Joey Dunlop still had to settle for second place behind the V & M Yamaha-mounted David Jeffries at the end of the 1999 Formula I TT. What made it all the more difficult to accept was that Dunlop had held the lead until the first pit stop when too much time was lost for even Joey to make up. Overall the 1999 TT provided no Irish winners for the first time since 1982, and for the first time in seventeen years Honda failed to win the Formula I race, something that neither Honda nor their most faithful servant accepted easily. They left the island already plotting their revenge. Joey Dunlop pictured at Guthrie's Memorial on the RC45 Honda.

Photo: Alastair McCook

137

One of the most impressive things I ever witnessed on a race track was Jim Moodie's opening lap of the 1999 Senior TT when he broke the outright lap record (that had stood since 1992) by seven seconds — from a standing start. No one expected that the record would be shattered as it was from a standing start, but that's exactly what the works Honda Glaswegian achieved. To be there and see it happen made the hair stand on the back of your neck.

The first sign that something special was unfolding was when Moodie was through Glen Helen and long gone on his opening lap before the commentary team had time to pick him up for the first time-check of the race. Moodie, riding with the Number 1 plate (plus a very small 2 in front of it to retain his lucky and preferred racing number 21), had no target to aim for. He simply let loose and what a sight it was to behold. He flashed past the Grandstand to clock a history-making 124.45 mph, but the pace in which he had ridden the opening 37¾ miles had taken its toll, and as his rear tyre started to slowly come apart, Jim Moodie had no option but to endure the bitter disappointment and retire from the race. It was fitting that his friend and fellow Scot Steve Hislop was spectating close to the point where Moodie abandoned the race and was on hand to offer his commiserations. Pictured on his way through Rhencullen on his historic record-breaking lap.

Photo: Alastair McCook

the 2000s

h Motorcycle and Car Club Ltd

elbourne Motors

dragee 100

Richard Britton, Adrian Archibald and James Courtney complete the podium at the Tandragee 100 in 2000. On the day Archibald produced an awesome display that secured a resounding hat trick for the Ballymoney rider, notching up the Tandragee 100 Feature race, as well as taking the Open and 600cc Regal races. It was a historic day for other reasons, Joey Dunlop's 125cc victory was his last win on home soil.

Photo: Alastair McCook

David Jeffries and Michael Rutter storm through Portstewart on the V & M R1 Yamahas during the 2000 North West 200 Superbike race. The 1999 North West 200 had been dominated by Jeffries. Twelve months on and the big Yorkshire man left the Triangle without a win, although he made it onto the podium three times. The Man of the Meeting was Michael Rutter who couldn't put a foot wrong as he took both Superbike race wins in style, and then started from the back of the grid to take the 600cc race win as well. Come the TT Jeffries more than made up for his North West 200 disappointment with a resounding hat trick on the Mountain circuit.

Photo: Alastair McCook

Photo: Alastair McCook

Joey Dunlop's Formula 1 TT victory in 2000 was the stuff that legends are made of. If you read about it in a *Boy's Own* adventure you probably wouldn't believe it. Since that day in June in the Millennium year thousands have proudly made the boast that "I was there" and I was one of them.

At the age of 48 Dunlop lined up on the Glencrutchery Road against a field who were on average roughly half his age. Men like Jeffries, Rutter, McGuinness and Archibald seemed the real contenders, on paper. Age was against Dunlop, and there were serious question-marks over whether Honda had provided their man with a bike that could match the opposition. It was no secret that Dunlop had only been allocated the Demon Vimto SP1 VTR 1000 Honda after he had made it clear to the team bosses that the Fireblade he had been given at the start of the season was not up to the job. The SP1 arrived in time to be given a run out at the Cookstown, and the initial signs seemed to bode well. Despite Joey taking pole for both Superbike races at the North West 200 the bike could not match the performance of the V & M Yamahas on race day, and Dunlop began to despair. The prospect of Honda having to stomach a repeat of their drubbing at the hands of V & M Yamaha twelve months earlier was unthinkable, but at times it seemed that Dunlop was the only one who took the task of restoring Honda's honour seriously. Eventually Honda put a one-off package together that included new forks, a trick works engine usually used by Kiwi World Superbike rider Aaron Slight, plus HRC technicians and Showa engineers to help put it all together and run it, but it was largely untried and still a gamble. On the day it all came together, and Joey Dunlop notched up his 24th TT victory and his first Formula 1 win since 1988. It was a simply stunning achievement that inspired and impressed all those who saw it.

On the Honda Fireblade at Aghadowey, Easter Saturday 2000.

First time out on the SP1 VTR 1000 in the rain at Cookstown, 2000.

All photos: Alastair McCook

Pictured on his way through the Highlander and on towards Greeba. The locals can only point and stare.

The Senior race is traditionally the race that brings the curtain down at the end of each year's TT festival: it is the final race of the week. In 2000 poor weather conditions dictated that the Senior TT would be postponed, prompting a mad scramble amongst those who had planes and boats to catch on the Friday evening to try and make last-minute changes to their travelling arrangements. The Saturday dawned bright and clear and in a delayed Senior TT David Jeffries stormed to complete his hat trick of wins for the week. Joey Dunlop had already sealed his own historic treble adding the Ultra Lightweight and Lightweight TT victories to his Formula 1 victory at the beginning of the week. Joey Dunlop finished the 2000 Senior TT in third place, and recorded a time of 123.87 mph on his sixth and final lap, his final lap around the circuit he loved so much. Pictured on the Demon Vimto SP1 at Tower Bends in his final TT.

Photo: Alastair McCook

No one has been more committed over the years towards achieving the goal of winning a TT than New Zealander Shaun Harris. He has suffered injury and near financial ruin in his quest. The flame-haired Kiwi finally realized a lifetime ambition in 2003 with storming performances that brought him wins in the 600cc and 1000cc Production races.

Pictured on Patsy O'Kane's Yamaha on the Mountain during the 2000 Junior TT.

Photo: Alastair McCook

Jeremy McWilliams has been the only Irish rider to seriously challenge at Grand Prix level since Tom Herron mounted a campaign with attitude during the 1970s. McWilliams has cut it with the best, riding in the 500cc class for the Joe Millar team, in the 250cc class riding for QUB Optimum Power Technology team, and as a works rider for Aprillia and Kenny Roberts' Proton. The highlight of a very distinguished career has to be his 250cc win at the Dutch TT in 2001. Pictured before the start at Stormont during the Millennium Motorsport Festival held on the August Bank Holiday 2000 **(right)**, and **(left)** entertaining the home crowd with a rolling burn-out at the foot of Carson's Statue.

Photos: Alastair McCook

Jason Griffiths leads Adrian Archibald through Wheelers Corner during their 2000 Ulster Grand Prix 600cc Supersport contest for second place. Archibald posted the fastest lap of the race at 122.405 mph to pip Griffiths to the flag. Griffiths was hardly off the podium all day, finishing runner-up behind David Jeffries in both Superbike races.

Photo: Alastair McCook

Adrian Archibald wheelies Chris Dowd's Honda down Carrowdore's main street during the 2000 event. It was the last time the race was held. The meeting was abandoned after Eddie Sinton's fatal accident and has not been held since then.

Photo: Alastair McCook

Strabane-based road racer James McCullough is no slouch himself when it comes to road racing. McCullough has mixed it with the best of them and a podium finish at the Manx Grand Prix is one of the highlights of his own career. But even road racers have their own heroes, and more often than not the man who inspired generations of riders was Joey Dunlop, and James is no different. This tattoo is his unique tribute.

Photo: Alastair McCook

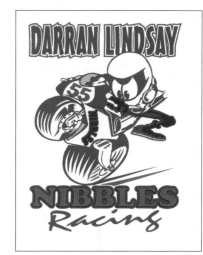

Another nail-biting 600cc race at Dundrod rounds Wheelers Corner, with Ian Lougher in charge of affairs from David Jeffries and Adrian Archibald. This one didn't have a happy ending. In the frantic sort-out between these leading three going into the last corner, Ian Lougher's TAS Suzuki clipped the artificial kerbing used to mark out the man-made chicane at Dawsons Bend. Gerry Allaway, flag marshal for that section of the circuit, was hit by Lougher's machine and died of the injuries he sustained.

Photo: Alastair McCook

<<Opposite page

Despite the fact that the racing administrators have shown a desire to phase out two-stroke racing, there remains a strong interest in the thoroughbred Grand Prix machinery. Not that many years ago the 250cc race would be the highlight of the day's programme, regularly producing frantic action and close finishes. Sadly the 2002 North West 200 only had room to run a race for 250cc bikes concurrently with the 600cc Class, effectively a race within a race. Despite the fact that the entry lacked numbers, the battle for the win between Ricky McCready and James McCullough went right to the wire with McCready steeling it out. Sadly Ricky McCready lost his life in a road accident the following year. Pictured on the run up Juniper Hill (top) and flicking into the start/finish chicane (bottom).

Photo: Alastair McCook

Danger is an integral component part of motor cycle road racing, there is no denying that. Those who take part and race are well aware of the risks involved. It doesn't make it any easier though when the worst fears become reality. Gary Jess was one of the finest prospects in road racing, and in 2002 claimed his first North West 200 podium finish with third place in the Production race. However, he was not allowed the chance to fulfil his potential or enjoy his success for long. Tragically the rising star lost his life in a first-lap crash at Cochranestown during the Ulster Grand Prix Superbike race. The fact that Gary Jess had finished in second place in the earlier 600cc Production and 400cc Supersport races in the day merely underlined the fact that he was poised on the verge of greatness when luck struck its cruellest blow.

Pictured on the grid before the start of the 2002 North West 200 Production race.

Photo: Alastair McCook

David Jeffries on the all-conquering TAS Suzuki during the 2002 Senior TT at Kepple Gate. TT 2002 saw Jeffries take an unprecedented third consecutive hat trick in a performance that completely dominated proceedings as he rewrote the record books and made mincemeat of the opposition all week long.

Photo: Alastair McCook

As well as the memorable 600cc races that have graced the Ulster Grand Prix over recent years, this 600cc clash during the 2002 Dundrod 150 was a bit special as well. Ian Lougher gets his head down and tries to break clear from the chasing pack of Darran Lindsay, Richard Britton, Adrian Archibald and Gary Jess on the uphill run from Irelands Corner towards Budore.

Photo: Alastair McCook

The year 2003 saw John McGuinness make his long-awaited Ulster Grand Prix début. McGuinness was already an experienced and respected competitor, listing amongst his achievements victories at the Isle of Man TT, North West 200, Daytona and a British Championship title. By the end of racing at the 2003 Ulster Grand Prix he had also bagged the Best Newcomer award, after a storming ride saw him claim a hard-fought 600cc Supersport third-place finish. Pictured at Tornagrough during the 2003 Ulster Grand Prix practice.

Photo: Alastair McCook

International
NORTH WEST 200

SUPPORTERS CLUB

MEMBERSHIP CARD
2005

Richard Britton leads Ryan Farquhar over Fentons Jump during the 2003 Mid Antrim 150 250cc race. Britton won the 600cc race but the day belonged to Farquhar who scooped the Man of the Meeting award via a resounding hat trick that included wins in the 250cc, Open and Challenge races.

Photo: Alastair McCook

Richard Britton at Ballaspur on his way to third place in the 2002 TT 400cc Supersport race. Britton had a smile on his face whether he won or broke down on the first lap — it wasn't an act, that's the way he was. His laid-back attitude and sense of humour made him hugely popular with the fans, never mind the fact that he was bloody fast. It was a massive blow to the racing world when Richard lost his life in a racing accident at the inaugural running of the Ballybunion Road Races in 2005.

Photo: Alastair McCook

John McGuinness rounds Kates Cottage and lines it up for the Creg during the 2002 Production TT. In 2004, 2005 and 2006 McGuinness set the Isle of Man alight with masterful performances that have seen him come of age with lap records and wins in the Junior, Senior, Formula 1 and Superbike TTs. He's come a long way from the days when he used to watch in awe as a lad and think, "I wouldn't mind a go at that".

Photo: Alastair McCook

In recent years frantic, close 600cc racing has almost come to be expected round Dundrod. This encounter in 2003 was no different and had the crowd gawping at the spectacle of a six-man dice on the road that defied belief at times. The line-up included all the usual suspects, Lindsay, Farquhar, Lougher, Britton, Griffiths and Archibald. All six lapped inside the lap record, and less than a second split the top four at the end. Lougher got the verdict from Archibald and Farquhar — but it was close. Farquhar and Griffiths give chase through the Flow Bog as Lougher, Archibald and Britton make their break for glory.

Photo: Alastair McCook

Fast, precise and stylish, Bruce Anstey tips into Dawsons Bend during the 2003 Ulster Grand Prix Production race, with Adrian Archibald in his wheel tracks. The positions remained the same to the flag.

Photo: Alastair McCook

Robert McCrum gives chase out of Bells Crossroads during the 2004 Tandragee
100. McCrum suffered serious injuries in an accident during the 2005 season which
resulted in the loss of his right foot. Never one to give up easily Robert has had a
special prosthetic limb fitted and in 2006 continued racing and winning.

Photo: Alastair McCook

The next generation of the Dunlop family get ready for Ulster Grand Prix practice in 2004. Robert's sons Samuel (a Manx Grand Prix winner in 2005), William and his younger brother and fellow racer Michael (in red jacket), share anxious moments on the grid before the off with crack Japanese road racer Jun Maeda. The status of all three riders as newcomers to the event is denoted by the orange bibs they are wearing. The weather (stair rods straight out of the heavens) is typical of Dundrod's own mini climate. Tragically Jun Maeda lost his life as a result of a practice crash during the 2006 Isle of Man TT.

Photo: Alastair McCook

Year after year the 600cc Supersport races at the Ulster Grand Prix are truly memorable epics, and this one in 2004 lived up to all expectations. The ten-wheel train that comprises Lougher, Anstey, Archibald, Britton and Farquhar thunders towards Dawsons Bend at just over 140 mph, inches apart and no quarter asked or given. One of THE all-time great races witnessed on the circuit was fought tooth and nail, as close as this for its entirety, but as the bunch approached Dawsons for the final time Ian Lougher appeared to have the win firmly in his grasp. In an uncharacteristic mistake Lougher ran wide, relegating himself instantly right out of the top three. Bruce Anstey took the victory and sealed a memorable hat trick of race wins on the day. The likeable Kiwi crowned his big day out at Dundrod with an absolute course record of 129.03 mph — the fastest lap recorded on any race circuit in the British Isles.

Photo: Alastair McCook

John Burrows (16) and Keith Stewart (92) in all sorts of trouble on the approach to Bells Crossroads during the 2004 Tandragee 100. The pair approached the right-hand turn shoulder to shoulder, hard on the brakes with neither prepared to give way. Both nearly crashed out — Stewart, with knee slider hanging off, took to the grass, overshot and sat it out for the remaining laps of the race; Burrows footed round the crossroads just about, but it had been a close run thing. The white and yellow blur in the foreground is all that can be seen of flag marshal Edwin Jackson as he takes evasive action.

Photo: Alastair McCook

Fast, precise and very spectacular. Darran Lindsay and Richard Britton side by side on Tandragee's jumps, May 2004.

Photo: Alastair McCook

The might and thunderous roar of the entire Superbike grid fills the road and rends the air as the 2004 North West 200 gets underway. Leading the charge is 3 Michael Rutter, 6 Bruce Anstey, 4 John McGuinness and 22 Denver Robb. Rutter dominated the day, and along the way made history, becoming the first rider on any British circuit to be clocked in a straight line at a speed of more than 200 mph. Just another day at the office for the HM Plant Honda rider.

Photo: Alastair McCook

Richard Britton's one-off partnership with the Rizla Suzuki team for the 2004 North West 200 was eagerly anticipated by the fans. It seemed on paper at least that Britton and the Suzuki, which had proved itself the bike to beat in the British Superbike championship, would be an unbeatable combination. The reality was bitter disappointment for Britton who struggled all week as the Suzuki defied every attempt to make it handle. In the end Britton was never on the pace or able to mount a serious challenge. Pictured on the grid during 2004 practice.

Photo: Alastair McCook

Ryan Farquhar notched up a brace of 600cc victories during the 2003 North West 200, but twelve months later had to settle for second and third place in his 600cc outings, as Bruce Anstey and John McGuinness split the spoils of victory between them. Pictured at full tilt on Portstewart's Mill Road.

Photo: Alastair McCook

(Top) Martin Finnegan crests Elders Jump during the 2004 Mid Antrim road races. Finnegan is a big, powerfully-built man, and his physical strength is put to full use in wrestling the bikes around tight, twisting, narrow public roads circuits. He is an ex-Motocross rider, which has helped him develop skills to do things as a road racer that not everyone can do. To see Finnegan in playful mood, approaching a road end at any one of the road races he contests from the TT down, and backing it in, the rear end of the big Yamaha trying to pass the front with wheels smoking, is truly quite a sight to see. He is the most exciting thing to happen to road racing in Ireland for years.

When you go to the Skerries 100 in July or the Killalane road races in September, the support for Finnegan is overwhelming; the expectations on him are immense. Martin Finnegan is the local boy, hailing from the small town of Lusk, which is barely a stone's throw from the circuits that host the two biggest races on the Southern Irish calendar. When the time of the year comes around for the Skerries or Killalane, the locals turn out in force to support their man. It seems everyone you meet, including the dogs in the street, are wearing Martin Finnegan T-shirts. For the locals there can only be one winner, and in 2005 Finnegan didn't disappoint. He returned to his home patch, psyched up and ready to go after taking his first TT podium finish (third in the Senior) a month earlier. In the process Martin Finnegan lapped the Isle of Man TT Mountain circuit at a speed of 127.014 mph, the fastest TT lap ever recorded by an Irish rider. Come race day at Skerries 2005 **(bottom)**, Martin Finnegan delivered the goods. He took a truly memorable hat trick of victories on his home circuit, but he had to ride hard for the wins. Martin Finnegan has talent, ability and courage in spades. He is poised to follow in the footsteps of the great Irish riders who have gone before him. He is Ireland's most exciting prospect.

Photos: Alastair McCook

The year 2005 was a good one for Raymond Porter with the Donegal man taking his first North West 200 win, and making the podium at the TT for the first time as well. On this occasion Porter doesn't have to worry too much about heat stroke, dehydration or being set upon by a plague of midges as the hailstones beat down during the 2005 Tandragee 100.

Photo: Alastair McCook

Michael Rutter arrived for the North West 200 in 2005 as the red-hot favourite to win both Superbike races. On race day Rutter didn't need long to realize he had a fight on his hands. The challenge came from Rutter's Honda-mounted British Superbike Championship rival Steve Plater, and as the pair reached Dhu Varren on the last lap, it was Plater out in front, with Rutter looking very much the runner-up. Cometh the hour, cometh the man, and with time running out, Rutter dug deep, made his move on the Coast road, nipping ahead of Plater and staying there to the flag.

Photo: Alastair McCook

With tongue out and every nerve focused on the task in hand, Kenneth McCrea rounds Dublin Corner during the 2005 Skerries 100 Grand Final. When was the last time you concentrated this hard then?

Photo: Alastair McCook

William Dunlop firmly established his own road racing credentials in 2005 with a 125cc win at Athea, closely followed in July with an emphatic 125cc victory at Skerries. Dunlop is the son of Robert Dunlop, but in a few short seasons has emerged from his father's shadow to challenge and beat the best in the game, fairly and squarely.

Pictured at Dukes Bends, Skerries, July 2005.

Photo: Alastair McCook

One of the great thrills you get photographing road racing is from how close you can get to the action. This photograph of John Burrows and Richard Britton was taken at the 2005 Mid Antrim 150. The bikes were so close that there was no need for a whopping telephoto lens and they still filled the frame.

Photo: Alastair McCook

The people who make road racing happen, the marshals and paying public, line up for the camera on a sunny Sunday afternoon at Kells, Co. Meath, July 2005.

Photo: Alastair McCook

Ian Lougher leads the 2005 Ulster Grand Prix Superstock race through Joey's Windmill. Lougher was untouchable, pulling away from the chasing pack with ease, whilst all hell broke loose behind him. Try as they might Lougher was on fire and simply was not going to be caught.

Photo: Alastair McCook

One of the most spectacular places I have ever looked at motor bikes through a lens is the blindingly-fast Budore Corner at Dundrod. This was the action during the 600cc Supersport race at the Ulster Grand Prix, 2005. McGuinness, Lougher, Archibald and Anstey, nose to tail, at over 150 mph. What is more remarkable is that Anstey had survived a massive off at Joey's Windmill in the previous Supersport race as he hunted down the eventual winner, Ian Lougher. Whilst most of us would have retired to the nearest pub to get over the shock of sliding along a country road on your back at over 120 mph, Anstey cadged a lift back to the pits, and was immediately back in the thick of the action on the 600cc TAS Suzuki in the following Supersport race.

It's a sight that is so, so impressive. Four riders travelling so fast that when you blink they have gone and already a mile distant. As you hear the engines get louder and come always nearer on their uphill run from Irelands Corner, the heart begins to beat a little faster, until by the time they roar through, yards from where you sit, the heart has leapt to your mouth which is by now like sandpaper. Nothing in the world compares to it or comes close, absolutely nothing.

Photo: Alastair McCook

Robert Dunlop announced his retirement from motor cycle road racing in 2004. He didn't stay retired too long. During his absence from the sport during 2005 Robert endured more pain on the operating table, opting to undergo surgery in order to have his right leg, so badly injured in his Isle of Man crash in 1994, straightened and lengthened. He returned to the track for the Cookstown 100 on 29th April 2006 in tenacious mood to line up against two of his sons, Michael and William, in the 125cc race. Despite leading from the start, a misfire dropped Robert out of contention for the win, leaving the way clear for William to open his account for the season, while Robert eventually claimed third place just ahead of Michael.

By that stage in the day Michael had already made his own mark on the meeting. In the Junior Support race Michael made his road racing début and claimed his maiden win with 22 seconds to spare.

The 2006 season has seen the 125cc class dominated by the Dunlops. Robert followed his son's Cookstown success with a breathtaking display at Tandragee one week later that saw him steal the win from under Darran Lindsay's nose on the final corner. Dunlop's win was greeted with delight by the fans, but it was only an appetizer for what was to follow a week later at the North West 200. Robert had been outpaced in practice and lined up on the grid in seventh place. After the opening lap it seemed that Robert's quest to win again on his home course was a lost cause as he languished well behind early leader and pole setter Michael Wilcox. As they started their last lap Dunlop lay second but with a mountain still to climb. The final circuit was one of the finest displays of Robert Dunlop's career, coming from nowhere to edge Wilcox out in the final yards. It was an emotional moment for all who were lucky enough to be there. The last time Robert Dunlop had won a race at the North West 200 had been twelve years ago. His treble in 1994 was followed weeks later by the accident that nearly cost him his life, and which finished his career as a Superbike rider. In the intervening years Robert has suffered more pain than most of us can imagine, and he has come back to win on his favourite track without his brother Joey at his side to offer his congratulations. Robert Dunlop has more talent in his little finger than an entire busload of Grand Prix superstars put together. He is gritty and determined and harder than nails. Robert Dunlop simply doesn't know the meaning of the word "quit".

As the 2006 season unfolded Robert Dunlop notched up win after win, including heart-stopping performances at Mid Antrim, Skerries and Dundrod.

Pictured leading sons 3 Michael and 6 William along with 86 Nigel Moore and 9 Mark Curtin at Gortin Corner, Cookstown 100, 29th April 2006.

Photo: Alastair McCook

As a sponsor Winston McAdoo has provided bikes over the years for some of the finest riders in the business. Names like Brian Reid, Alan Irwin, Bob Jackson and Ryan Farquhar have all piloted the McAdoo missiles to success. The 2006 season began with a new face in the McAdoo team in the form of Yorkshire's Ian Hutchinson. The 25-year-old vindicated his selection for the team with a resounding win on his first outing as he held off the double threat of Raymond Porter and Cameron Donald to claim the Cookstown 100 600cc race. If luck had been on his side Hutchinson would have left the Orritor circuit with a hat trick of wins under his belt. He led both Superbike races for most of the distance only to lose out on the last lap on both occasions. A 600cc victory at the North West 200 more than made up for the disappointment. One of the most exciting talents to arrive on the scene for many a day.

Photo: Alastair McCook

There is no finer place to be than Tandragee on race day. By the traditional date for the Co. Armagh road race spring has just turned the corner into early summer, the hedgerows are in full leaf and the racing is usually out of the top drawer. The year 2006 was no exception, with Australian Cameron Donald emerging as the sensation of the meeting as he stormed to wins in the Open race and Tandragee 100 feature race. If that wasn't enough Donald hoisted the absolute course record to 106.20 mph from a circuit he had never set eyes on before!

The Open race gets underway with the front row comprising from left to right: 35 Trevor Ferguson, 71 Davy Morgan, 86 Cameron Donald, 3 Adrian Archibald, Martin Finnegan (blue and white Arai helmet), 10 Raymond Porter and John Burrows.

Bruce Anstey is a superstar. On the big occasion he delivers the goods over and over again. He is fast, brave and stylish, and he does it all with a smile on his face. His performance at the 2006 North West 200 was once again exceptional. Anstey was hardly off the podium all day, blitzing his way to Superstock and Supersport victories, as well as a Superbike runner-up spot and Supersport third place. Pictured at Dhu Varren leading Michael Rutter during the De Walt Performance Tools Superbike race.

Photo: Alastair McCook

Steve Plater has been trying to win at the North West 200 for more years than he can remember. During the year 2006 it all came good for the likeable Plater who claimed an absolute course record of 124.11 mph as he stormed to victory in both Superbike races on board the HM Plant Honda. Pictured on Juniper Hill showing no less than 100% commitment with knee slider planted firmly on the road.

Photo. Alastair McCook

John McGuinness was the undisputed star of the 2006 Isle of Man TT festival. McGuinness hoisted his career tally of TT wins to 11 with a resounding hat trick as he claimed victory in the Superbike, Supersport and Senior TTs. Along the way McGuinness set new race and lap records in every class he won. The highlight of the week for many was McGuinness' storming performance on Senior Friday that ended the week with McGuinness claiming the distinction of first man to lap the Mountain circuit at over 128mph, before he opened the taps on the HM Plant Honda to push the outright lap record to a staggering 129.451 mph.

McGuinness is pictured accompanied by his son Ewan on his way to collect the spoils of victory from TT legend Giacomo Agostini, whilst the assembled throng of fans, team personnel and gentlemen of the press show their appreciation. A very special moment in a career that has already seen McGuinness elevated to the status of legend.

Photo: Alastair McCook